Publications
of the
Minnesota Historical Society

RUSSELL W. FRIDLEY, *Director*
JEAN A. BROOKINS, *Assistant Director*
for Publications and Research

Museum Exhibit Series No. 2

Prepared by the Education Division
of the
Minnesota Historical Society

WHERE TWO WORLDS MEET

the great lakes fur trade

CAROLYN GILMAN

with essays by Alan R. Woolworth, Douglas A. Birk, and Bruce M. White

MINNESOTA HISTORICAL SOCIETY • ST. PAUL • 1982

Managing editor: Ellen Green
Catalog design: Earl D. Gutnik
Artifact photography: Eric Mortenson
Cover: Skin coats modeled on the European cloth coats sold by traders were made by the Ojibway, Cree, and particularly the Red River métis. For further information on this coat, see page 107.

This book is printed on a coated paper manufactured on an acid-free base to ensure its long life.

10 9 8 7 6 5

Library of Congress Cataloging in Publication Data:

Gilman, Carolyn, 1954–
  Where two worlds meet.

  (Museum exhibit series; no. 2) (Publications
of the Minnesota Historical Society)
  Bibliography: p.
  1. Fur trade—Great Lakes region—History—
Exhibitions. 2. Axe industry—Great Lakes region—
History—Exhibitions. 3. Great Lakes region—
Commerce—Europe—History—Exhibitions. 4. Europe—
Commerce—Great Lakes region—History—Exhibitions.
5. Minnesota Historical Society—Exhibitions.
I. Minnesota Historical Society. II. Title.
III. Series. IV. Series: Publications of the
Minnesota Historical Society.
HD9944.U46G744   380.1′456753′0977   82-2089
                    AACR2
International Standard Book Number: 0-87351-156-5

Printed in Singapore

CONTENTS

FOREWORD

The exhibition that this catalog documents came into being as a result of a longstanding interest in the North American fur trade on the part of the Minnesota Historical Society. That interest has been demonstrated over the years in a series of distinguished publications, including the well-known books of Grace Lee Nute and works by Solon J. Buck and by Theodore C. Blegen.

Even more tangible evidence of the Society's interest can be seen in its persistent efforts to mark, preserve, and restore sites associated with the fur trade in Minnesota. These have included such places as Forts Beauharnois, St. Charles, and Renville, posts at Mendota, Big Sandy Lake, and Traverse des Sioux, and the fully reconstructed North West Company wintering post on the Snake River. Most important, however, in terms of both historical significance and long-term Society involvement has been the Grand Portage. Efforts that began in the early 1920s eventually resulted in designation of the site as a national monument and in a long series of archaeological investigations.

The Society reached farther afield in the early 1960s when it initiated a 13-year underwater search of historic canoe routes along the Canada–United States border. Conducted in close cooperation with Canadian organizations, this project produced a veritable treasure trove of trade goods, remarkably preserved in the clear, icy waters where canoe accidents had dumped them centuries earlier.

In 1965 the Society organized the first of a continuing series of international conferences on the North American fur trade. Two subsequent gatherings at Winnipeg in 1970 and 1978 broadened Canadian and British participation. Planning for the fourth conference, held at Grand Portage, Minnesota, and Thunder Bay, Ontario, in October 1981, provided the impetus for undertaking a major museum exhibition. The Society conceived this as an opportunity both to make available to scholars the artifacts accumulated over the years of archaeological work and to explore the importance of material culture in the study of the fur trade. A photographic preview of the exhibit was displayed at the conference; the artifactual exhibit itself opened at the Society's museum in St. Paul on February 9, 1982.

In undertaking this project the Society drew upon talents and experience of two generations of fur trade scholarship within its own staff. Those who provided ideas, contacts, knowledge, and critical appraisal include: Robert C. Wheeler, Alan R. Woolworth, Douglas A. Birk, Rhoda R. Gilman, Bruce M. White, Curtis L. Roy, Dennis Hoffa, and W. Roger Buffalohead. Assistance in making selections from the Society's collections was given by Marcia G. Anderson, Robert M. Clouse, and other members of the museum and archaeological staffs. Every member of the Society's Education Division staff contributed at one point or another, but particular responsibility was carried by Nicholas Westbrook, curator of exhibits, Earl D. Gutnik, designer, Patricia A. Gaarder, museum assistant, and Deborah E. Swanson, research assistant. Ellen Green edited the exhibit text and supervised production of the catalog. The photographs are the work of Eric Mortenson. The one who pulled it together—curator of the exhibit and author of the main text in this catalog—is Carolyn Gilman.

Thanks go to the National Park Service for permission to use artifacts recovered at the Grand Portage National Monument. Other institutions lending materials are the Royal Ontario Museum, the Oregon Historical Society, and the St. Louis County Historical Society. The Hudson's Bay Company, Old Fort William, and the Public Archives of Canada provided particular assistance, and the exhibit is enhanced by the gift of two Scanamurals from the 3M Company Foundation. A maritime history grant from the National Trust for Historic Preservation enabled the Society to clean and stabilize artifacts recovered during the underwater search, many of which are included in the exhibit. Catalog production was made possible by financial assistance from Minnesota Power & Light Company (Duluth); Duluth, Missabe and Iron Range Railway Company (Duluth); Julia Marshall (Duluth); Caroline Marshall (Duluth); Northwestern Bell Telephone Company (Duluth); Reserve Mining Company (Silver Bay); First National Bank of Duluth; First Bank—Duluth; First Bank Duluth—West; and Potlatch Corporation (Cloquet).

A particular debt of gratitude is owed to Alan R. Woolworth, who generously shared a vast fund of information concerning the history of the fur trade and the material remains that document its life, its economy, and its impact upon larger areas of human culture.

RHODA R. GILMAN
ASSISTANT DIRECTOR FOR EDUCATION

A novel kind of commerce ruled this land from 1600 to 1850. Europeans traded their manufactured goods for the furs of the American Indians. People from two different worlds met, and their goods and ideas mingled. Neither culture was ever the same again.

WHERE TWO WORLDS MEET

Carolyn Gilman

What is the importance of the fur trade? This question seemed easy to answer 50 years ago. To historians of the early 1900s, the fur trade was one step in the inevitable march of Western civilization deploying its forces to conquer barbarism. The grand old apologists of colonialism saw the fur trade as the first outrider of progress preparing to transform a sleeping, savage land. With fascinated approval they chronicled the exploits of the great explorers who paved the way for the railroads, cities, and highways of modern America. It was easy to explain things in those days.

Nowadays we answer the question only with more questions. We are no longer so certain that the process by which this land was settled and stripped of its finest natural resources was admirable, or that our culture has any more right to call itself civilized than the American Indian cultures before it. In the wake of Hiroshima and Vietnam, imperialism has lost some of its savor.

Without its nationalist aura, the fur trade does not appear so clearly related to the process of settlement that came after it. If the fur trade set the pattern, why is not the Ottawa River a major commercial thoroughfare? Why are not Mackinac, Grand Portage, and Prairie du Chien the New York and Los Angeles of the Midwest? Why did fur traders of the 1790s lobby for an independent Indian state where traditional ways of life (the Indians' and their own) might be preserved? And why did the end of the 19th century find more traders' descendants on Indian reservations than in corporate boardrooms and state legisla-

tures? In fact, the evidence suggests that the fur trade, through much of its 300-year history, was actually antithetical to settlement.

What, then, *is* the importance of the fur trade? Since the 1950s some new answers have been suggested. New methods of historical inquiry sent researchers back to business records and vital statistics to ask what was really going on. How were prices set? Do supply-and-demand equations work for the fur trade? How did family networks affect trade? Were animals really depleted? What role did ceremony and gift-giving play? Simultaneously, Indian activism jolted some historians out of their ethnocentrism, making them realize that they had been ignoring half of the activity of the fur trade—the half initiated by Indians. Application of anthropological studies to fur trade history produced information about Indian trade networks, economic conventions, and hunting methods.

By now the fur trade has been described in many ways: as a model of the extractive industries that systematically depleted our continent of most of its natural resources, as a mechanism of acculturation, and as an example of intercultural economics, to mention only a few.

It was all of these things, of course. But if we distill these descriptions down to one word expressing why the fur trade should be important to every schoolchild, truck driver, and bureaucrat in North America, the word would be *communication*. The fur trade is an example of how two radically dissimilar cultures establish a common ground of understanding without sacrificing their unique characteristics and without annihilating one another. The fur trade is a story of how people act when they meet the Other: the stranger, the puzzling change in accepted wisdom, the rapid onslaught of the future. People invent solutions, some predictable and some astonishingly creative, but all very human. Above all, in the face of pressure people cling to their humanness and adopt strategies to make the forces of change respect them.

Carolyn Gilman, curator for the exhibition, Where Two Worlds Meet: The Great Lakes Fur Trade, *has worked for the Minnesota Historical Society's Education Division exhibits department since 1978. Her work in the Society's Publications and Research Division from 1975 to 1978 included co-authorship of* The Red River Trails *(1979),* co-editorship of The Northern Expeditions of Stephen H. Long *(1978), and editorship of the journal of James Stanley Goddard in* The Journals of Jonathan Carver *(1976).*

American Indians had a variety of strategies for incorporating the Other. They used political and family institutions to co-opt the European strangers and fit them into Indian molds. But the most successful strategy was both symbolic and practical: the exchange of belongings. Trade goods were the alphabet letters of the language that broke the barriers between Europe and America. Laden with cultural information, the tools of everyday life projected telling though unintended portraits of their makers. The social conventions facilitating this exchange of objects carried a second level of information and formed a prototype for political, ceremonial, sexual, and familial interaction. Understanding was not just a by-product of commerce: It was the lifeblood.

The fur trade was thus an exchange of information: information about technology, about social organization, about human nature. But once we say this, there are few other generalizations to make about the fur trade. The specific messages conveyed by trade goods were subject to a myriad of variables. Time, geography, tribal or national affiliation, and the relationships between participants each had a bearing on communication happening in a particular trading transaction. The fur trade was not a homogenous whole. The first step towards understanding it is to be aware that methods of trade changed over time, and that networks of political-commercial relationships in North America changed over space. The challenge is to untangle the confusion of variations and identify some of the broad patterns.

It is helpful to think of the evolution of fur trading methods in three phases. During the first phase European participation was somewhat tenuous and passive. The main burden of organization was on Indian tribes. Europeans tended to establish themselves in single locations (such as Montreal, Fort Orange, or York Factory) and depended on Indian trading parties to travel to them. As trade became more complex, Indian nations specialized as fur producers or middlemen. The former hunted while the latter handled the transportation and bargaining. Indian groups competed for access to hunting grounds in one direction and trade goods in another. There was also great rivalry for the powerful middleman position. The interaction of Europeans and Indian traders had profound political and ceremonial as well as commercial overtones. Tribes bargained as groups, not as individuals. Indians wielded great power, since they gathered and transported the furs. European goods traveled far inland in the hands of Indian traders, but Europeans had little control over the profits reaped from their

resale. Europeans frequently tried to sidestep Indian monopolies that exploited them.

In the second phase Europeans moved into the interior, taking on more steps in the trading process and preventing their customers from organizing to control trade. Europeans took over much of the transportation of goods inland, but they still relied on Indians to hunt and process pelts, and to supply food and information. The act of trading became more decentralized, although commercial cliques and monopolies often controlled supply and transportation. European traders dealt with Indians as individuals, not as groups. Most Indians no longer specialized as middlemen and hunters, but they did specialize in support activities such as canoe building and agriculture. Conflict frequently arose between competing groups of traders. Trade lost many of its political and ceremonial overtones. Marriage between Indians and Europeans became of great importance, as did understanding of Indian customs and languages. This phase met initial resistance from Indian middlemen standing to lose their profitable position to European encroachment, from established European merchants threatened by the decentralization of trade, and from governments that saw control over commercial and political relations with Indian tribes slipping away. The second phase was welcomed by Indians for the convenience and lower prices associated with nearby traders and by individual European entrepreneurs who saw new opportunities for making a living. Settlement was not a motive of this European movement west; in fact, settlement was diametrically opposed to the interests of traders in the second phase.

In the third phase the fur trade became a tool of expanding industrial nations and a precursor to settlement. Though not usually long-lived in any particular area, this phase was the one on which judgments about the fur trade's importance and social effects have often been based. In the United States, it was intimately associated with the process of treaty-making and was characterized by a high level of government involvement. A fur company wielded increasing political power derived from its economic influence over the Indians. Fur traders and companies exploited government annuity payments to tribes and rapidly diversified into lumbering, mining, land speculation, general merchandising, and transportation. The white market—settlers, soldiers, missionaries, government agents, and white trappers—expanded. The power of long-established fur trading families was undermined, and family ties with Indian tribes were discouraged. Hunting skills no longer gave the Indians a base of power; in some places white trappers even replaced the Indian work force. Resentment and conflict between Indians and Europeans became more frequent. This phase led to denial of Indian access to the land, in turn spelling the end of the fur trade.

The evolution of these phases had little to do with game depletion. Scarce animal resources plagued all three phases; the problem was generally solved by relocation of hunting grounds, by conservation practices, or by altered demand. (For example, muskrat replaced the disappearing beaver as the primary felt-producing fur in the 1830s.)

The succession of these phases also seems independent of the political and ethnic affiliations of the European participants. National variations in trading methods existed, of course; but their importance has been exaggerated. One common myth was that the French, the first Europeans forced into phase-two trade, were uniquely suited to deal with Indians on a one-to-one basis. Similarly, since the British at Hudson Bay clung to phase-one methods, this mode was thought to be peculiarly British. The untruth of both assumptions is clear. The French operated a phase-one system as restricted as the British for more than half a century, until the failure of their middlemen partners endangered their wealth. When faced with ruinous competition, the British undertook a phase-two method of trade as aggressive as the French. And when a Scottish-Canadian merchant class took over the French trade network in Canada in the 1760s, there was no change in approach beyond that provided by increased capital and decreased regulation. Trading networks had a life and growth rate independent of national, political control.

In geographical terms, the Great Lakes fur trade was shaped by the interaction among four trading networks determined by transportation routes and tribal alliances. The first and largest was the Algonquian Indian system on the St. Lawrence River and Great Lakes proper. Set up by the Iroquoian-speaking Huron in the 1640s, this network was later exploited by the Ottawa and the French. The transportation routes and methods pioneered there were also used after 1763 by British traders working out of the St. Lawrence Valley. At the end of the 18th century this trading system, represented by the North West Company, had reached its tentacles to the Mississippi and Missouri valleys, the Rocky Mountains, the Hudson Bay drainage basin, and the Mackenzie River headwaters. The War of 1812 split the terri-

tory between Britain and the United States. North of the international border the system was absorbed by the merged North West and Hudson's Bay companies. South of the border it became the province of the American Fur Company.

The second major trading system lay north of the Great Lakes and was ruled by the Assiniboine and Cree around Hudson Bay. The British Hudson's Bay Company was the main European participant. This network had the scantiest population and the richest fur supplies. Although for many years European traders never pressed inland from the shores of Hudson Bay, Indian middlemen traveled along the waterways far to the south and west to trade for furs with tribes of the Great Plains and the Athabasca region. South and east of the bay, this trading network constantly impinged on the Great Lakes network, fueling the national rivalries of the British and French for a century.

The third major trading system affecting Great Lakes history was the Iroquois network. From their homeland in upper New York state, the Iroquois tried to establish themselves as middlemen between the Dutch and English on the Hudson River and the western tribes. Although often frustrated in their attempts to penetrate the French-Algonquian network to the north, the Iroquois had much success in trading with Ohio Valley tribes. On the whole, however, the English-Iroquois trading system was simpler than the others, with the Iroquois serving primarily as hunters rather than as middlemen. In the 18th century American traders used Iroquois routes and ties as their main avenue into the west.

A fourth trading system, originated by native-born French traders living near present St. Louis, appeared in the late 18th century along the Mississippi River. Although this system was in part an offshoot of the St. Lawrence–Great Lakes trade, the St. Louis traders shipped furs out through New Orleans as well as through Montreal during the early 19th century, offering parent concerns in Canada increasing competition. When British traders were barred from United States territory after the War of 1812, this trading system took over exploitation of the American Rockies. In the Missouri Valley it was absorbed again into the Great Lakes system through the expanding American Fur Company.

From 1600 to 1850, each of these trading systems evolved through the three phases of development described earlier. But their evolution was seldom simultaneous and always fraught with regional variations. For instance, the Great Lakes–Algonquian system began changing from phase one to phase two as early as the 1670s, but the Hudson Bay system did not reach this stage until the 1770s. Similarly, although the Iroquois trading system was becoming a phase-three precursor to settlement in the late 1700s, the Hudson Bay system did not take on this role until the 1860s and 1870s. The interaction of these variations accounts for some of the complexity of Great Lakes fur trade history.

When all these factors are taken into consideration, it becomes clear that a kettle traded to a Huron band in the 1640s was the catalyst for a wholly different set of social interactions from one traded to an Ojibway band in the 1840s. In the 1640s, the Indians and Europeans met as strangers. The setting was formal and public; the participants met at least partly as representatives of their nations. The exchange was embedded in an Indian cultural milieu. It was partly a ceremony for gaining personal prestige, partly a treaty cementing political alliances with European nations. Exchange was conducted by a mostly male commercial clique within the tribe that thereby gained power (and, no doubt, created dissension). Never far from the surface was the intent of gaining honor, alliance, and wealth for the entire tribe by reselling merchandise under circumstances similarly charged with connotations of prestige and politics.

The 1640s kettle was not just a utilitarian item. Adopted into a Huron system of beliefs, it had a ceremonial role (for instance, as grave goods) and an animating spirit. To the Europeans it was animated by an exchange value that gave it life quite apart from its usefulness as a tool. The kettle would wreak social transformations far more significant than its technological innovations.

A kettle traded to an Ojibway in the 1840s was a very different matter. The exchange was informal and private, near an Indian village. Trade was between individuals, either male or female. The trader and the Indian might be related by marriage, perhaps several generations back. The other formal tie between them was not politics but debt. Partly due to an altered ecological balance, the fur trade was no longer a road to riches or power; neither trader nor hunter could make more than a bare living. They were forced to seek other sources of income: the Indian through sale of his or her land, the trader through general merchandising, land speculation, and treaty awards. The trader no longer represented a nation; instead he worked for a company. Yet, to the subsistence trader, the fur trade was less a business than a way of life.

The 1840s kettle was not an innovation, but a symbol of cultural conservatism. Long ago it had been adopted into Indian culture, either for itself or transformed into other shapes. It symbolized generations of wild rice harvests and maple sugar processing. It had been cut into knives and arrowheads and had adorned clothing as tinkling cones and gorgets. Now it bore messages from the outside world of mass production and concentrated application of energy. These messages were foreign to trader and Indian alike. The trading post was the locus of a conservative subculture that reached the height of its individuality on the very eve of its demise.

The change that took place in the 200 years between the trade of the two kettles was an essential ingredient of the fur trade; it had to be, since the exchange of information was so rich. Every viable society absorbs new information and adapts. The rapid changes in North American life were not degeneration of any supposedly "pure" Indian culture, but signs of vitality and responsiveness to an influx of new data. What we must never lose sight of, however, is the fact that cultural adaptability always exacts a price in individual lives and happiness.

The influx of information and the changes it wrought were by no means confined to North America. Knowledge of Indian lifeways brought about profound change in European attitudes toward history and human development. Information from America was behind the concept of natural law and inherent rights that contributed to the democratic ideology of the French and American revolutions. The Indians' liberalizing effects on the European mind included the genesis of cultural relativism and the demise of narrowly Biblical interpretations of the past. It was no accident that European mores based on private ownership and the class system came under fire during the greatest influx of new anthropological evidence.

Written sources tell us about the kinds of communication that people were aware of. But what of all the unspoken information passed unintentionally from person to person along with the axes, beads, guns, and furs? What of the nonverbal exchanges? For these we must turn to archaeology and to artifacts that still carry the evidence encoded within them. This book is based on an exhibit that makes some of these material sources available. Artifacts do not yield dates or policies or places. Their information is allusive, symbolic, mythic. They cannot replace written sources; neither can written sources speak entirely for them. The objects must tell their part of the story themselves. ■

The Great Lakes fur trade started along the Atlantic Coast when Europeans and Indians found that each had something the other wanted. The Indians valued the Europeans' knives, hatchets, kettles, and beads. The Europeans valued the Indians' animal skins. They traded, and both thought they were getting something for nothing.

The worlds of the Europeans and Great Lakes Indians were very different. One was becoming a capitalist, industrial civilization; the other was a society of farmers and hunters. They had different possessions and very different ideas about them. When they traded belongings, they traded part of their worlds as well.

At first they judged each other by their goods. Europeans called the Indians savage because they used tools of stone rather than metal. The Indians in turn disdained the traders' mad competition for furs. The French must be a poverty-stricken people, a Micmac Indian told a priest, as "you glory in our old rags and in our miserable suits of beaver which can no longer be of use to us."

In Europe, the more goods a person owned, the greater his prestige. Possessions carried messages about their owners' status, work, sex, age, and taste. But Indians admired people not for accumulating goods but for giving them away. Cooperation and sharing were necessary for survival; people who hoarded, endangered others. Goods were exchanged for need and honor, not for profit.

WHERE TWO WORLDS MEET

The people of the Countrie came flocking aboord, and brought us . . . Bevers skinnes, and Otters skinnes, which wee bought for Beades, Knives . . . Hatchets, [and other] trifles.
—Robert Juet, 1609

The English have no sense; they give us twenty knives like this for one Beaver skin.
—a Montagnais Indian, 1634

1. ENGRAVED CARTOUCHE, 1777. A trading transaction was represented on William Faden's "Map of the Inhabited Part of Canada, from the French Surveys." C-35062/Public Archives Canada.

ALL THE WORLD WAS ALIVE

The Great Lakes Indians knew that tools had souls. They knew it because their tools came to them from the living world of the woods. The only thing that kept a family of hunters alive was empathy with their natural surroundings. Since everything they owned, ate, and wore came from the woods, they had to balance their use of a variety of resources, so that no single one was overused.

The Indians' relationship with the woods was very personal. To them, every animal and plant had habits and opinions of its own. Some Indians burned an animal's bones after eating the flesh to avoid offending the being who had given up its life. They offered tobacco to a dangerous rapids so it would let a traveler pass by. Fishermen set nets far enough apart that they would not be jealous of one another. People were buried with their favorite things so the spirits of the objects would accompany the spirit of the owner. Indian culture did not just respect nature: It was shaped by nature.

These objects show the intimate bond between their makers and the resources of the environment.

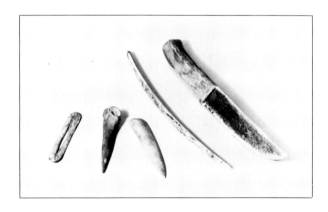

2. BIRCH-BARK BOX, late 1800s? Great Lakes Indian artists achieved colorful designs by embroidering birch bark with dyed porcupine quills. This box (11-3/8" long by 6-1/2" high by 6-5/8" wide) is covered with floral and double-curve quillwork patterns and lined with pink cotton fabric. Although probably of late date, the box represents an early style of art. Its tribal attribution is uncertain, but it is of Micmac or Malecite style. See color page 58.

3. HORN SPOONS, undated. Buffalo- and cow-horns were soaked until pliable, then shaped and carved. These spoons, reportedly of buffalo horn, include one from the Red River area (left, 5-3/4" long by 2-1/4" wide) and one with no provenance (right, 6-1/2" long by 2" wide).

4. BONE TOOLS, late 1700s to late 1800s. Every part of an animal killed by Indians was used; bones became tools like these. From Mandan villages in North Dakota are a shuttle (left, 3-3/8") for weaving netting and three ground and polished awls (center, 3-3/4" to 8-3/8" long) used as leather punches, ornaments, daggers, or pottery engravers. Iahbiance, a Cass Lake Ojibway, used a method common among Canadian Ojibway to make the skinning knife (right, 9-1/8") from a split rib bone.

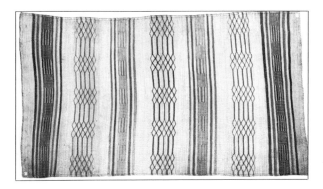

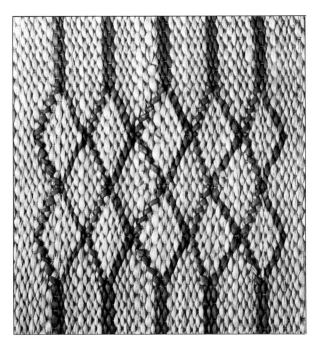

5. PIPE BAG, early 1900s? Plains Indians wrapped brightly dyed porcupine quills around two parallel threads to create geometric designs on this creamy hide bag. Collected by artist Frederick Wilson, the bag (5-3/8" wide by 28" long) has a hide fringe.

6. POUCH, c.1900? Great Lakes Indians used beaver fur for their own clothing, blankets, and accessories as well as for trade. This fur and skin pouch (11-1/2" by 6-5/8") is decorated with fringes and long, quill-wrapped hide strands with metal cones and feathers. Its reverse side is of cured hide embroidered with seed beads. The bag may be of eastern Dakota origin.

7. REED MAT, late 1800s. For centuries Ojibway Indians made mats by weaving dyed bulrushes with basswood fibers on a wooden frame. In this mat, green and purple rushes form a diamond or "ottertail" pattern. This example (53" wide by 93-3/4" long) was collected at Leech Lake, probably in the 1890s.

8. DETAIL OF REED MAT, late 1800s. See above.

9. POTTERY JAR, undated. Pottery was important to Woodland and Mississippian Indians in the Great Lakes region, and the art persisted even when imported metal pots and ceramics became available. This example (4-1/2" high by 4-1/8" diameter) made of clay mixed with crushed clamshells represents pottery of the southern United States. It was collected in the late 1800s.

10. WOODEN BOWL, undated. This bowl (15-7/8" diameter by 4-3/4" high) carved from a tree burl may have been used for food. The raised portion of the rim may be a stylized effigy; the top edge bears two brass tacks. Lead-inlay double-barred crosses appear on two sides. Robert O. Sweeny pictured similar bowls being used by the Dakota in the 1850s and 1860s.

11. WILLOW BASKET, early 1900s. Pliable twigs of yellow peeled and red blighted willow were woven in strips to form this melon-shaped container. The handle and rim were made of another kind of wood. The basket (8" high by 7" wide) was collected from the Grand Portage Ojibway in 1930 by ethnologist Frances Densmore, who identified it as "old style."

12. BIRCH-BARK BASKET, c.1890. This birch-bark basket sewn with basswood bark strips was decorated inside by scratching off the bark's thin sap layer when it was fresh from the tree. When immersed in hot water the scratches remained light, but the sap layer turned dark brown. Amateur ethnographer Fred K. Blessing, who purchased the item (15-3/4" long by 10" wide by 4-3/8" deep) at Mille Lacs, identified it as Eastern Woodland.

LORDS OF ALL THE DRY LAND

Europeans did not see themselves as part of an interlocking, animate universe. Instead, they were commanded to control nature—to harvest what was useful and subdue what was not. Tools were weapons in the battle against the environment.

When Europeans first met the Indians, most trade goods were handmade in private homes. But during the fur trade years (1600–1850), the Europeans' struggle to conquer their world took a turn in their favor. This was the time of the Industrial Revolution. New sources of power and new technologies transformed Europe from an agricultural, peasant society to an industrial, capitalist one. By 1850, most trade goods were manufactured by steam- and water-powered machinery. Nature had been harnessed, if not subdued.

These artifacts from the three main eras of trade show the changes occurring in European technology.

God said to them, "Be fruitful and multiply, and fill the earth and subdue it; and have dominion over the fish of the sea and over the birds of the air and over every living thing that moves upon the earth." —Genesis, 1:28

FRENCH GOODS

From 1600 to 1763 traders in the Great Lakes region were mostly Frenchmen trading with the Huron, Ottawa, and western Algonquian tribes. The French quickly learned that the Indians were highly skilled in working leather and wood. But since they lacked metals and textiles, these soon became staples of the fur trade.

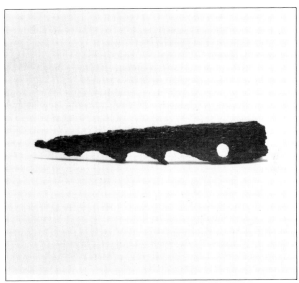

13. CLASP KNIFE BLADE, mid-1700s. This French clasp knife blade (5-1/8" by 1-1/8") was excavated at Fort St. Charles on Lake of the Woods, dating 1732–1750s. Such a folding blade was commonly attached to a bone, horn, or wood handle by a pin through the hole at the base. Some folding blades were controlled by a spring in the handle, though there was no spring mechanism found with this blade. Its maker's mark is two columns of letters reading "B Z L O P" and "I A I N A" with an "A" at top center.

14. HARPOON POINT, mid-1700s. This iron implement excavated at French-era Fort St. Charles on Lake of the Woods is an exact copy of bone harpoons made by North American Indians. Perhaps used to spear large fish, the point (5-3/8" by 3/4") has a hole in the tang for attachment to a line.

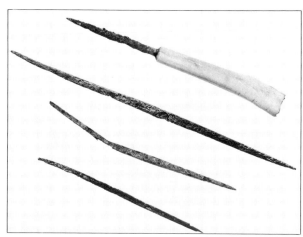

15. GUNFLINTS, undated. Flintlock guns, introduced by the French to Great Lakes trade, were ignited by a spark created when a flint struck a steel frizzen. These round-heeled, wedge-shaped, golden flints were found by the Quetico-Superior Underwater Research Project in Basswood River. Of large measure (1-1/4" to 1-5/8" long by 1" to 1-3/8" wide) they may have been used with rampart guns or fire steels.

16. ARROWHEADS, mid-1700s. Europeans quickly learned to cater to Indian technology, and metal arrowheads were among the earliest trade goods. These examples (1-3/8" and 7/8" long) were found at Fort St. Charles, a French establishment on Lake of the Woods dating 1732–1750s.

17. FELLING AX, late 1600s. This French ax of uncertain origin probably came from eastern Ontario. Hand-forged of iron, it has an oval eye and three maker's marks in the form of a circle divided into eight wedges. The ax (7-1/2" long by 3-7/8" across blade) was found by the Royal Ontario Museum, Toronto.

18. AWLS, early 1600s to 1776. Indian craftsmen added handles to iron or steel awls sold by traders for piercing holes in leather and bark. The top example, of iron with a bone handle, measures 3-7/8" and dates to the early 1600s. The bottom three, also of iron, were excavated at Fort Senneville (occupied 1704–1776) on Montreal Island in the Ottawa River. Lent by Royal Ontario Museum, Toronto.

19. GLASS BEADS, early 1600s. Although they were probably not made in France, these "star" or "chevron" beads were typical of French trade goods. Layers of red, white, and blue glass were ground away in patterns to reveal the colors beneath the surface. The small beads (left, 1/4" long) have no provenance, while the larger beads (right, maximum 1-1/2" by 7/8" diameter) are from Halton County, Ontario. Lent by Royal Ontario Museum, Toronto.

20. GLASS BEADS, early 1600s. These irregular, spherical glass beads, excavated from an eastern Pennsylvania site dating to the early 1600s, are now iridescent with age. The beads average 1/4" in diameter. See color page 67.

21. "JESUIT RINGS," mid-1700s. These French rings were not necessarily worn or distributed by missionaries, but they may have been mass-produced for trade. Made of brass, they bear cryptic inscriptions, possibly of religious origin. These specimens were excavated in the 1970s at Fort St. Charles, a French establishment on Lake of the Woods dating 1732–1750s. All are under 7/8" in diameter.

22. KETTLE, 1640–1650. The marks of a French coppersmith's hammer are preserved in the surface of this kettle from a Neutral site in Lincoln County, Ontario. As he hammered out the metal, the smith apparently pivoted the kettle, producing rows of marks around its circumference. The kettle (16-1/2" diameter by 9" high) has a rolled rim and dog-earèd lugs fastened with rivets. Lent by Royal Ontario Museum, Toronto.

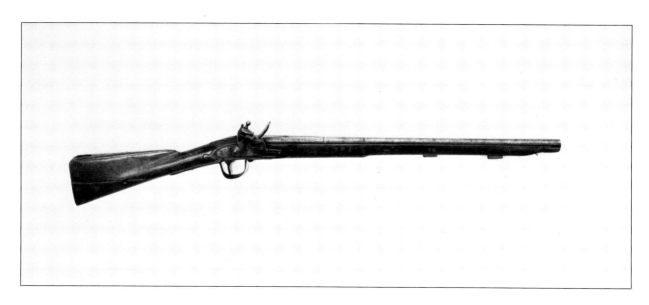

BRITISH GOODS

The British replaced the French as the primary suppliers of goods for the Great Lakes fur trade after 1763. Their imports reflected England's commercial ties with an expanding empire: rum made from West Indian sugar, tobacco grown in Virginia, linen cloth from Ireland. Woolen cloth, knives made in Sheffield, and iron tools made in Birmingham and Manchester reflected the development of English industries. Silver jewelry and iron tools were produced by craftsmen in Montreal.

23. FLINTLOCK GUN, mid-1800s. The Barnett Company of London was a prominent manufacturer of trade guns for at least 80 years in the 19th century. The owner of this gun (44″ long) sawed off the barrel and decorated the stock with tacks. The stock is bullet-damaged and its butt plate, ramrod, and tacks are missing. The lock plate is stamped "Barnett/London" with a tombstone fox and initials "EB." The barrel (28″ long) is stamped with a crowned "GP" and "V" (London Gunmakers Company marks), a "24" indicating musket ball size, a pennant mark, and "J.E.B.," the initials of John Edward Barnett, head of the Barnett Company, 1850–1875.

24. GUNFLINTS, undated. These square-heeled dark gray gunflints have a "blade" or "platform" shape introduced into England in the late 1700s. The flints have parallel top and bottom surfaces, easy to clamp securely between the jaws of a flintlock cock. All measure under 1″ by 1″.

25. AWLS, late 1700s. The wood or bone handle of a straight awl (bottom) tended to split under pressure. So manufacturers introduced a number of ways to seat them. The two "offset" or "crooked" awls are a type often found at British-era sites. The zigzags anchor the awls firmly in their handles. These awls (3-1/8") are from the North West Company depot at Grand Portage.

26. FIRE STEELS, late 1700s. Mass-produced in cities like Sheffield, England, these forerunners of matches were struck against flint to make sparks for starting fires. The oval one (top, 3-3/4" by 1-3/4") found by the Royal Ontario Museum in the French River, Ontario, has an unidentified maker's mark of two lions rampant facing left. The D-shaped steel (bottom, 3-1/8" by 1-1/2") excavated at Grand Portage has a handle at the top and a striking surface at the bottom.

27. TRADE AX, late 1700s. The light, durable British trade ax (also "half ax" or "ice ax") was produced in huge numbers. This example (6-1/4" long by 3-1/2" across blade) is marked "BAR" or "RAR," probably for a Birmingham or Sheffield manufacturer. It was one of a case of 29 iron axes found at Boundary Falls on the Winnipeg River by the Quetico-Superior Underwater Research Project. It is corroded from exposure.

28. KNIVES, late 1700s. Britain led the world in making cutlery in the late 1700s. At top is a common Revolutionary War–era folding clasp or pocket knife (6" by 3/4") with rivets for attaching a bone or wood casing to the handle, found at Hat Point on Grand Portage Bay. Excavated at the North West Company depot, Grand Portage, were two standard multipurpose blades with straight backs (bottom, 8" by 1-1/8" and 8-5/8" by 1-3/8").

29. SILVER CROSS, 1767–1809. Silver jewelry introduced by British entrepreneurs soon became a popular trade item. Like most trade silver, this pendant (5″ long by 2-3/4″ wide) was made in North America rather than in Europe—in this case by Robert Cruickshank (maker's mark "RC") of Montreal. It was found in 1963 at an old Ojibway ricing camp on Big Sandy Lake, near the site of a North West Company post established in 1794.

30. GLASS BEADS, late 1700s. Excavated at the British-era depot at Grand Portage, these restrung glass beads probably date from the post's principal years of use, 1785–1803. While most of these examples (1/16″ to 1/4″ diameter) are seed beads, some are cylindrical cane beads, and at least one is a mandrel-wound barrel bead. See color page 66.

31. RINGS, early 1800s? These two small brass finger rings (5/8″ diameter) were excavated at Grand Portage in 1963. The center bezels are of clear (left) and green (right) glass, and both were originally flanked by four blue sets.

32. TWO METAL KETTLES, late 1700s? The symmetrical, finished appearance of these kettles (7″ diameter by 3-1/4″ high) testifies to the development of factory metal-working techniques. Probably made from standard-sized copper or brass sheets pounded into shape with a waterpowered trip-hammer, the kettles were smoothed in a foundry and possibly finished on a waterpowered lathe. Nested for compact shipping, they were found in the French River in Ontario.

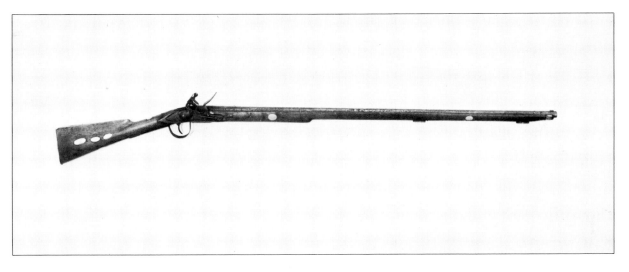

AMERICAN GOODS

American traders moved into the Great Lakes fur trade after the War of 1812. With them came the products of American factories: knives from one of America's first waterpowered cutlery works at Green River, Massachusetts, traps made by a machine process developed at Oneida, New York, and cotton grown in the American South. Guns made with interchangeable parts flooded the Indian market. New, efficient manufacturing methods produced an abundance of goods the Indian trade had never known before.

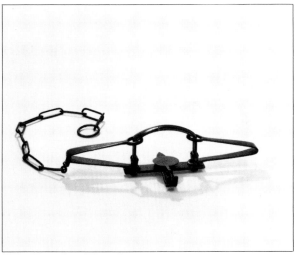

33. FLINTLOCK GUN, mid-1800s. The owner of this gun (55-1/2" long) apparently laid 12 German silver ovals in its stock. The marks on the lock plate indicate the gun was made by the Philadelphia manufacturer George W. Tryon or his son, Edward K. The Tryon firm was a supplier of trade guns to fur companies such as that of Pierre Chouteau, Jr., in St. Louis, as well as to the United States government, which distributed them as treaty and annuity payments. The barrel is stamped with tree, bush, pheasant, and star designs.

34. TRAP, mid-1800s. Sewell Newhouse, of the utopian Oneida Community in New York, first developed methods for mass-producing metal traps, and from the 1820s on, his brand was one of the best on the market. This hand-forged beaver-type trap (13-5/8" by 4-7/8"), probably dating from the 1850s, has "S. Newhouse/ Oneida Community" stamped onto one of the springs. It has square nuts at the bottom of the jaw posts.

35. BRASS KETTLE, late 1800s. In 1851 a Connecticut inventor patented a method for forming brass kettles on a lathe. Spun brass kettles soon replaced the earlier varieties made with trip-hammers, both in Indian and white markets. This example (8-1/4″ high by 11-3/4″ in diameter) was donated along with the papers of Abram M. Fridley, agent for the Winnebago Indians at Long Prairie, but its provenance was not given.

36. FIRE STEELS, mid-1800s? Many fire steels sold by American traders were mass-produced in England. This popular oval type was held through the middle and struck on either side. These three examples (3″ long by 1-1/2″ wide) are from the Ojibway community at Grand Portage. One bears the maker's mark "GAE" or "GRE."

37. GREEN RIVER KNIFE, late 1800s? In the 1830s John Russell introduced waterpowered trip-hammers for forging blades and a production line to increase output at his new knife factory in Greenfield, Mass. Soon he rivaled the Sheffield cutlers. Stamped "J. Russell & Co./ Green River Works," his knives were distributed by fur companies such as that of Pierre Chouteau, Jr. This skinning knife (10-3/8″ by 1-3/8″) has a black handle, possibly of gutta-percha. Lent by Alan R. Woolworth.

38. AX, mid-1800s? This heavy ax probably was forged by an American blacksmith before being sold to an Ojibway Indian. Archaeologist Jacob V. Brower recovered the ax (7-3/4″ long by 3-3/4″ across the blade) at Mille Lacs Lake around 1900.

39. PIPE TOMAHAWK, mid-1800s? Pipe tomahawks, introduced about 1700, were traded and used in ceremony well into the 1800s. This one's steel head (5-3/4″ long) has an octagonal bowl and a teardrop-shaped eye. Its wooden haft (13-3/8″ long) is wrapped at the base with a steel strip. Henry M. Rice, who traded with the Winnebago for the Chouteau Company in the early 1840s and who was later involved in various treaties and Indian affairs, donated it in 1885.

40. GLASS BEADS, mid-1800s. American fur traders continued selling beads from Amsterdam and Venice into the 1800s. These beads (1/4″ to 5/8″ long), typical of those traded from the 1830s to the 1850s, were excavated in St. Paul in 1906. See color page 67.

41. ARMBAND, mid-1800s. Silver ornaments became less common trade items as they were replaced by newly developed and less expensive alloys and processes like silver plate. German silver, an alloy of nickel, copper, and zinc, took over much of the Indian jewelry market. This nickel silver armband (2-3/4″ long by 1-3/4″ wide by 1/2″ thick), embossed with an undulating zigzag, is said to have belonged to the Dakota leader Little Crow (d.1863).

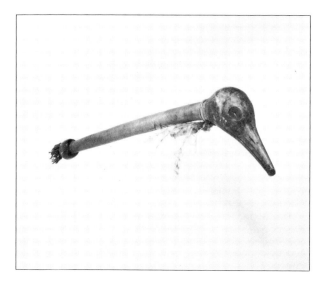

VOICES IN THE WOODS

To the Algonquian tribes living around the Great Lakes, the woods were full of consciousness. The beaver spoke a language of his own; the bear was a messenger from heaven; angry animal spirits brought death and disease. Animals were not inferior species put on earth for mankind's use; they were spiritual beings and relatives of man.

Ojibway clans traced their genealogies back to animal ancestors. Lynxes, wolves, bears, and others gave their traits and alliance to succeeding generations. Indian artists expressed their interdependence with animals by fashioning tools, weapons, and clothing in the shapes of the residents of the woods.

42. EFFIGY PIPE, undated. This pipe shows two birds on the base and four human faces on the surface of the upright bowl. Carved of steatite, the Ojibway-style pipe (7-5/8" long by 3-3/8" high) was accompanied by a quill-decorated wooden pipestem when it was acquired at Akeley between 1895 and 1910.

See color page 60:
43. EFFIGY PIPE, undated. This pipe (9" long by 4-1/8" high) is carved of spotted pipestone (catlinite) in the shape of a bird's head. Inlaid with lead, it is of Dakota style, probably dating to the latter part of the 19th century.

44. CLUB, early 1900s? A bird effigy forms the head of this wooden stick. It has red-painted eyes and neck and an orange beak. A short cotton strip is tied around the neck, and feathers are attached. The handle's bottom has a tassle of cotton string. Collected at the Ojibway White Earth Reservation, this piece (18-1/4" long by 5-7/8" at head) resembles Plains Indian dancing sticks.

45. HORN SPOON, late 1800s. The handle of this Dakota horn spoon is carved into a bird with an open beak. Where the handle meets the bowl, it is wrapped in porcupine quills. James C. Ferguson (1875–1955), who spent his early years at various army posts in the Dakotas, collected this spoon (9" long by 3-1/8" across bowl) at Fort Totten, N.Dak.

46. PIPE, undated. A bear with outstretched paws lies on the surface of this wooden pipestem. The bowl is of pipestone. The pipe (11-1/2" long by 1-1/2" high) was collected in the early 1900s by anthropologist Gilbert L. Wilson, and is probably a Plains Indian piece.

47. EFFIGY PIPES, undated. These two heads are carved of gray sandstone quarried in southern Minnesota and Wisconsin. One (left, 4" long by 1-1/2" wide by 2" high), a serpent whose mouth forms the pipe bowl, contained tobacco remains when found by archaeologist Jacob V. Brower at Bear Island, Leech Lake, in the 1890s. The dog or bear head (right, 2-1/2" long by 1" wide by 1-1/2" high) has a hole for inserting a stem under its chin. It was collected by Newton H. Winchell from the Ojibway in Sherburne County in 1908. It resembles pipes found at Madeline Island, Wis., and St. Ignace, Mich.

48. UMBILICAL CORD CASE, late 1800s. This turtle-shaped hide case (4" long by 2-1/4" wide) was used to keep a child's umbilical cord. Heavily embroidered with seed beads, it was collected in the 1890s from Dakota Indians at the Cheyenne River Reservation, S.Dak.

49. WAR CLUB, undated. The carved wooden shaft of this club (39-3/4" long) ends in a bird's head with brass tack eyes. The handle's incised designs include a straight line ending in a pipe image and a wavy line ending in a V. Spear blades (3") are set into slots in the haft and held with metal pins. It was collected by John B. Sanborn, a member of the 1860s Indian Peace Commission formed to negotiate with central Plains tribes.

Previous to the discovery of Canada . . . this Continent . . . may be said to have been in the possession of two distinct races of Beings, Man and the Beaver.
—David Thompson, 1840s

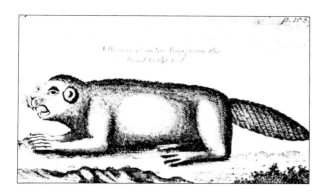

"THESE SAGACIOUS ANIMALS"

Europeans were astonished by the abundance of wildlife in the new world. Like the Indians, they saw themselves reflected in the animals. But unlike the Indians, they admired only the animals' cleverness and industry, and not their spiritual power.

The beaver, an animal nearly extinct in Europe, fascinated the amateur naturalists who came to North America. Wild stories claimed that these animals had a knowledge of democratic government, architecture, and engineering. But accurate knowledge of the seasonal habits of animals was necessary in order to harvest the great quantities of fur needed for trade. By the late 1700s, European observations were becoming less fanciful.

50. *A BEAVER 26 INCHES LONG FROM THE HEAD TO THE TAIL*, 1703. This fierce beaver is an engraving from Baron de Lahontan's *New Voyages to North-America.*

51. BEAVERS, 1738. The supposed habits and hunting of beavers are shown in this engraving from Claude Le Beau's *Avantures . . . ou, Voyage Curieux et Nouveau.*

52. *BEAVERS BUILDING THEIR HUTTS*, 1760. Beavers carry lumber on their shoulders up the ramparts of their fortress in this detail of an engraving from an English book, *The World Displayed; or, A Curious Collection of Voyages and Travels.* Humanities Research Center, The University of Texas at Austin.

53. *THE BEAVER*, 1664. Dog-like beavers build a dam in this detail of an engraving from François Du Creux's *Historiae Canadensis seu Novae-Franciae.*

See color page 70:
54. *LA CACCIA DEI CASTORI*, 1760. European concepts of how to catch beavers are shown in this Italian tinted engraving. Hudson's Bay Company.

Trade built a bridge between the two worlds of Europe and America. Let us follow two artifacts as they travel across that bridge to the trading post where they are to be exchanged. Their journey is just one example of how the trade might have taken place.

Picture a year in the late 1700s: In Europe, a blacksmith fashions an ax for the Indian trade. In America, an Indian hunter sets out to catch a beaver.

In the Great Lakes fur trade Indians did almost all of the hunting. But their ideas about hunting were very different from those of the Europeans who bought the fur. To the Indians of the Great Lakes, hunting was a spiritual exercise as well as a necessity. Much of the work was done before the hunter set foot out of his home. In dreams he heard the animal guardians telling him where to find the game. He sought the animals' permission to kill them, and if he were worthy, the animals granted it. An Indian family lived from day to day by the gracious self-sacrifice of the animals.

To European traders the woods were not alive. They could not hear the beaver talk. They wanted the Indians to hunt their animal relatives for profit. The Europeans never understood how much they were asking.

JOURNEY OF A FUR

HUNTING

55. *SPEARING MUSKRATS IN WINTER,* 1853. This engraving by Charles E. Wagstaff and Joseph Andrews from a watercolor by Seth Eastman shows Indians hunting in the upper Mississippi River area.

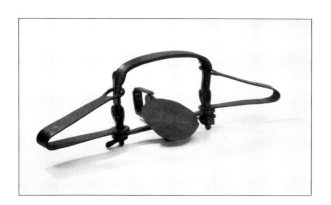

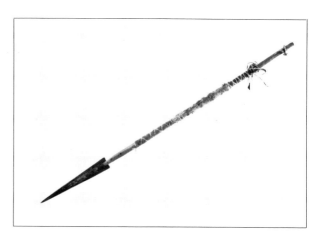

TOOLS OF THE HUNTER

Finding the animal, not killing it, took the greatest skill in hunting. European hunting tools did not ease the search; they merely made the kill simpler.

Moose, elk, and bear were dispatched with guns, bows and arrows, or even lances. Smaller game was caught in snares or (later on) metal traps. Muskrats were speared in their huts in winter. The ice chisel was most often used for hunting beaver. In winter, when fur was thick, hunters cut holes in the ice near a beaver lodge and lowered nets through the holes. Then one man broke apart the lodge with an ax. The animals, trying to escape, got caught in the nets under the ice. The hunters quickly pulled them out and dashed out their brains with the chisels.

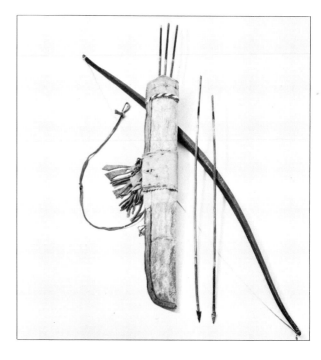

56. METAL TRAP, early 1800s. Laboriously assembled by blacksmiths, this kind of hand-forged iron trap was so expensive that fur traders often lent rather than sold them to Indian hunters. This example (25-1/4" long by 9-1/4" wide), probably used to catch large game like lynx and wolf, was made in Jamestown, Va., and carried west to Indiana, Iowa, and finally Minnesota. It was donated by the great-grandson of the original owner.

See color page 71:
57. *CANADIAN INDIANS SPEARING BEAVER,* 1830–1834. This watercolor attributed to Peter Rindisbacher shows the use of spears and axes in winter hunting. State Historical Society of Wisconsin.

58. SPEAR, undated. Spears like this Plains Indian piece dating to the 1800s were used in hunting, ceremony, and war. The iron or steel head has a tang that fits into a groove in the wooden shaft and fastens with two rivets. The shaft is wrapped with strips of red wool, muskrat fur, and leather thongs decorated with feathers. The 57-3/4" spear has a 15-1/4" by 2-1/2" blade.

59. BOW AND ARROWS, late 1800s. Guns never completely replaced the cheaper, easy-to-repair bows and arrows. This Dakota bow (44-7/8" long) from Fort Totten, N.Dak., is stained red on its outer surface and black inside. The stiff rawhide quiver (28" long by 4-1/8" wide), which may be Ojibway, has red-and-green painted designs and is decorated with seed beads and fringe. Two of the arrows (26-5/8" to 29-5/8" long) have metal tips secured with sinew.

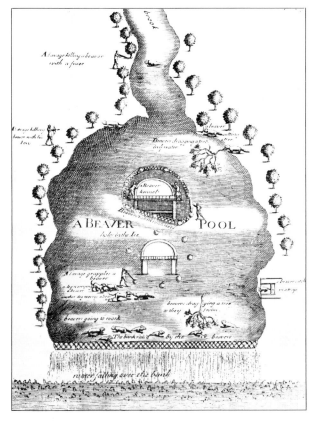

HUNTING THE BEAVER

This quaint picture, drawn by a French trader about 1703, shows the many different methods of hunting beaver. In the center, hunters cut holes through the ice. In summer, other hunters shoot the beavers outright with guns and arrows. On the right is a trap—not a metal trap, but a deadfall trap designed to crush the animal with heavy logs. Baited with fresh aspen or poplar twigs (the beavers' favorite food), traps and snares were set along the beavers' land paths.

The most destructive hunting method, lower left, was to break down the beaver dam and drain the pond. The beavers, unable to escape to the water when their lodge was broken open, were caught on the pond bottom by hunters' dogs.

60. MUSKRAT SPEARS, early 1800s? Muskrats and fish were often killed with iron spears mounted on long handles. The one with a single barb (15-1/8″ long) was found at Lac qui Parle, the site of a trading post and mission in the 1830s and 1840s. The one with a conical point and two barbs on opposite sides of the shaft (14-3/8″ long) is identical to late 18th century spears found by the Quetico-Superior Underwater Research Project.

61. *A BEAVER POOL*, 1703. Both winter and summer hunting methods are shown in this engraving from Baron de Lahontan's *New Voyages to North-America.*

62. TRAP, late 1800s. The design of steel traps remained largely unchanged throughout the 19th century. This machine-made Newhouse "No. 1" trap (8-5/8″ long by 3-3/8″ wide) was identified by the donor as a muskrat trap, but it could be used for mink, marten, and other small animals as well. Archaeologist Jacob V. Brower collected it at the Ojibway community of Mille Lacs.

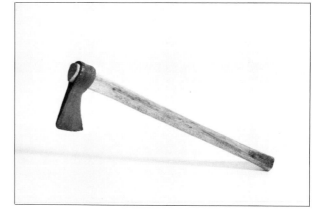

63. *THE BEAVER,* 1865. This accurate representation of a beaver was drawn by John R. Chapin and engraved by Joseph S. Harley for Sewell Newhouse's *The Trapper's Guide.*

64. ICE CHISEL BLADES, late 1700s. Wrought iron ice chisels were mounted on handles up to 6 feet long. Broad, flat chisel blades (left and center, 15-7/8" by 1-7/8" and 18" by 1-7/8") were made by hammering an iron bar into a sharp edge. The left one has indentations for hafting. A skewed point (right, 16" by 3/8") was formed by cutting through a bar at an angle. The outside chisels are from a set of 39 found in the Winnipeg River by the Quetico-Superior Underwater Research Project. All are corroded.

65. AX, undated. Axes were essential for opening beaver lodges, chopping through ice, cutting the pieces for deadfall traps, and many other hunting jobs. Henry D. Ayer collected this axhead (6" long) deeply marked "NB," probably around Mille Lacs Lake. The haft (25-1/4") is modern.

66. SNARE WIRE, late 1700s and modern. Wire was essential for snaring animals; unlike string or cord, it could not be chewed apart. This thin 18" length of brass wire twisted into loops on both ends was recovered by the Quetico-Superior Underwater Research Project in the Basswood River. At left is a coil of modern snare wire for comparison.

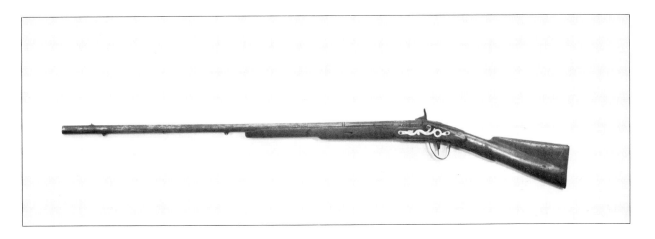

WOULD YOU BUY THIS GUN?

Advantages
- A gun is more efficient than a bow and arrow: It shoots a longer distance, more accurately, with greater power.
- The loud report gives you a powerful psychological advantage in war.
- There is great prestige in owning a gun.
- Using a gun is fun.

Disadvantages
- Gun barrels sometimes blow up, killing or maiming the hunter.
- When you are hunting animals that run in herds, one loud report scares away the animals for miles around.
- Guns are unreliable. If you get your powder wet, run out of shot, or lose your gunflint, the gun is useless.
- Guns are habit-forming: Once you have one, you are dependent on the trader for shot, powder, gun worms, files to repair the gun, and spare parts.

67. TRADE GUN, 1834–1862. The lock plate of this percussion gun (50-3/4" long) bears a tombstone fox and "H.E. Leman/Lancaster Pa." for its maker, a prolific supplier of trade guns to fur companies and the United States government after 1834. On its barrel (36" long, probably sawed off) are imitations of Birmingham proof marks and the initials "I.F.T." On the butt plate is a "P." A rosette design is carved on the stock, which is partly missing. Parker I. Peirce acquired it, probably from the Dakota, during the Dakota War of 1862.

68. GUN EQUIPMENT, various dates. To keep a gun working, a hunter needed equipment like this: (counterclockwise from upper left) a leather shot pouch and powderhorn with vent pick (for cleaning the touch hole) and powder measure, lead shot, musket balls, gun worms (attached to the ramrod for cleaning the barrel or removing unused charges), gunflints, and metal files for repairing broken parts.

Forging a bar of hot iron into the shape of an ax, a blacksmith in Birmingham, England, was acting as part of a complex industrial system. Before the iron ever came to the blacksmith, it passed through the hands of many specialized workmen. Miners brought ore from the earth; smelters refined it in a blast furnace. Each time the metal changed hands, a company made a profit. The ax enriched many Englishmen before it became an article for trade.

Europeans did not rely on the variety of the ecosystem as the Indians did. By specializing they changed their environment beyond recall. They had found that a farmer could raise more food if he concentrated on one kind of crop and that a herder could raise a greater flock of one type of animal. Manufacturers also specialized. One person seldom made a tool from start to finish. This led to the development of factories where dozens of people gathered to make a single kind of item more efficiently. As a result, Europeans could produce great quantities of axes in a very short time. And they all looked much the same.

JOURNEY OF AN AX
MANUFACTURING

69. *AN IRON WORK, FOR CASTING OF CANNON,* 1788. English landscape painters portrayed the awesome and demonic beauty of industrialization in engravings like this one by Wilson Lowry of River Severn, Shropshire, from a painting by George Robertson. Paul Mellon Collection, Yale Center for British Art.

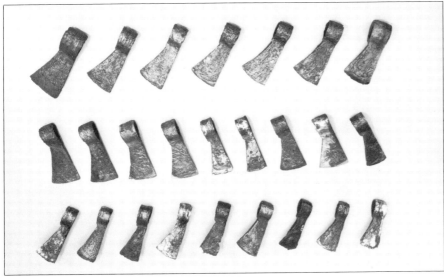

70. *THE INSIDE OF A SMELTING HOUSE, AT BROSELEY, SHROPSHIRE,* 1788. This engraving by Wilson Lowry of a painting by George Robertson evokes the spirit of the Industrial Revolution. Paul Mellon Collection, Yale Center for British Art.

71. TRADE AXES, late 1700s. These 25 hand-forged axes were in a shipment of 36, probably all made by the same manufacturer, found by the Quetico-Superior Underwater Research Project in the Basswood River. Each is made from a long, flat iron slab that was wrapped around a bar to form the eye, then welded together to form the blade. Corroded from exposure, the axes are in a graduated range of sizes from 5-1/4" long by 2-1/8" across blade to 7" long by 3-1/8" across blade.

After the beaver was caught and skinned, the fur was either sold directly to a European trader or traded to an Indian middleman. In the latter case, the fur entered an established network of trading ties: America had been a busy emporium of trade long before Europeans set foot upon the continent. Farming tribes traded food with hunting tribes; woodland dwellers traded forest products to people of the plains. Valuable shells and minerals traveled thousands of miles.

The customs and contacts formed by early Indian commerce determined the course of the fur trade. As tribes competed for access to trade items and for the influential position of middleman in the trade, European goods infused new life into the Indian trading networks. When Europeans followed Indian traders west, they moved along the same routes, used the same transportation, and used the trading customs of their predecessors.

On the next page are some of the articles Indians might have traded among themselves.

JOURNEY OF A FUR

TRADING

72. *INDIANS TRADING*, c.1860. A trading transaction between Indians was portrayed by Robert O. Sweeny in this ink wash on paper.

73. SHELLS, undated. Seashells were avidly traded by inland tribes. Top to bottom are: a shell once owned by the Ojibway of Ponsford; two shells from a cache at Crane Lake; two dentalium shells from the Pacific Coast found at Sandy Lake; a fossilized shell (possibly found locally) from Fort Clark, N.Dak.; and three salt-water cowries prized by the Ojibway for their religious symbolism. They range from 2-5/8" by 1-5/8" (top) to 5/8" by 1/2" (bottom).

74. COPPER TOOLS, 3000 B.C.–1 A.D. The remote ancestors of American Indians mined and worked Lake Superior copper into tools much like later trade goods. Copper was still traded when Europeans arrived. Left to right are a knife blade (9-1/4" long) from Dane County, Wis.; a tanged spearhead (8-7/8" long) given by Indians at the Lower Brule Agency, S.Dak., to Dr. Nathan R. Hurd in the 1890s; a socketed spearhead (9-3/8" long); and an awl (7-1/4" long) found near Montello, Wis.

75. PIPESTONE, various dates. Minnesota catlinite was traded all over North America. Clockwise from right are an unworked block, probably from the pipestone quarry; three beads (under 1" long) found on the banks of the Fox River at Neenah, Wis.; nine cylindrical beads with large central holes (3/4" long by 3/8" diameter, average) from Minnesota; a pipe bowl (5" long by 3-1/4" high) found at Wounded Knee, S.Dak.; and a pipe bowl (1-1/2" wide by 1-7/8" high) found near Stockbridge, Wis. All are prehistoric except the typical 19th-century Dakota pipe on the left.

76. KNIFE RIVER FLINT, prehistoric. Chert quarried near Knife River, N.Dak., and traded through the Missouri and Mississippi valleys, made excellent projectile points and knives. This projectile point (left, 2-3/4" by 1") was found in Itasca County in the late 1800s. The scraper blade (bottom) and six chert flakes (upper right, all under 2") are from Minnesota.

THE CANOE

Since prehistoric times, trade in the Great Lakes area was carried on by canoe. Without this Indian invention a large-scale fur trade would have been impossible here. The birch-bark canoe was perfectly designed for the rough waterways of North America: light enough to be carried over portages, sturdy enough to hold heavy loads of cargo, and easy to repair with materials available anywhere in the north woods. But, because the canoe had to be paddled and portaged, labor was the greatest expense of the trade.

In the canoes of the savages one can go without restraint, and quickly, everywhere, in the small as well as large rivers. So that by using canoes as the savages do, it would be possible to see all there is, good and bad, in a year or two.
— Samuel Champlain, 1603

77. *CANOE OF INDIANS,* 1857. Eastman Johnson made this oil sketch of an Ojibway family in a birch-bark canoe at Grand Portage. St. Louis County Historical Society, Duluth.

78. *VIEW OF CANOE PARTY AROUND CAMPFIRE,* c.1865. Travelers, camped for the night, inspect the seams of their birch-bark canoe by torchlight in this oil on canvas, one of a series painted by Frances Ann Hopkins while traveling through the Great Lakes with her husband Edward, a Hudson's Bay Company employee. C-2772, Picture Division, Public Archives Canada.

79. CANOE REPAIR KIT, late 1700s and undated. Holes or cracks in a birch-bark canoe were patched or sewn together with spruce root *(wattape)* threaded through holes punched in the bark with canoe awls. These awls (8-5/8″ and 6-5/8″ long) are from the North West Company depot at Grand Portage. The cracks were then caulked with pine pitch (shown in an 8″ by 6″ birch-bark tray), which was softened by boiling and mixed with powdered cedar charcoal.

The new ax was sold to an English company acting as the agent and supplier for a fur trading company, and soon it was on the road to a great port like Liverpool, Glasgow, or London. There the ax entered the sphere of a commercial empire stretching around the globe.

Goods from South America, Asia, and Europe came to the ports of Britain for shipment to North America. Brilliant vermilion from the Orient, Brazilian tobacco, Holland twine, Venetian beads, knives from Sheffield, and other exotic wares joined the ax. All were evaluated, insured, and packed in bales and kegs. The agent company sealed the knots of the bales with its insignia stamped in lead so no one could pilfer the goods.

JOURNEY OF AN AX
TRADING

80. *GRAND PANORAMA OF LONDON, FROM THE THAMES*, 1849. This detail from a panoramic engraving, probably sold as a tourist souvenir, shows part of the Thames River waterfront near the London Docks.

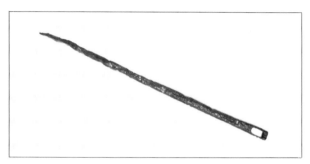

FEEDING THE FACTORIES

The fur trade was only one sign of the great change occurring all over the world from 1600 to 1850. With explosive speed, European peoples spread out to conquer, colonize, and trade with the undeveloped regions of the globe. When they came to Africa, Asia, and America, Europeans reasoned that here were inexhaustible sources of raw materials for their industries, and that the inhabitants of those regions would buy manufactured goods in return. Eager to extract resources from uncharted areas, European merchants expanded their trade networks and their knowledge of the world.

81. LEAD SEALS, 1770–1820. Packing firms attached lead seals embossed with their insignia to baled goods prior to shipment, to identify or protect the merchandise. The Quetico-Superior Underwater Research Project found one (left, 1-1/4" diameter) marked by the packing firm of Isaac Whieldon, London (fl. 1790–1820), and another (right, 1-3/8" diameter) marked "WA," possibly for London packer William Alchorne (fl. 1770).

82. BALING NEEDLE, late 1700s. Heavy needles like this one (5" long) were used to sew through sailcloth and waterproof tarpaulin required for packing furs and goods. Excavated in the kitchen area of the North West Company depot at Grand Portage, it is made from a round steel rod hammered into a diamond-shaped cross section at the point, now broken.

83. *CASA DA FABRICA DA TABACO*, 1792. This watercolor shows a Brazilian tobacco factory where workers prepare twist tobacco like that sold by the foot or yard in North America. First tobacco leaves hang to dry. Then two workers (back) strip and stem the leaves as others (front) twist them into ropes with a spindle. Finished twists are stored against the walls (left) until they are shipped out in 90-pound rolls.

84. BRAZIL TOBACCO, undated. Indians north of the Great Lakes preferred expensive Brazilian tobacco to the cheaper American-grown kind. Traders had to import it via a roundabout route from South America to Portugal, to Britain, and finally to North America. It was shipped in large cigar-shaped packets called *carrots* and long ropes called *twists*. The spiral twisting of this piece (4-3/4" long by 7/8" diameter) can still be seen.

85. *SHEFFIELD FROM THE ATTERCLIFFE ROAD,* 1819. The seat of the English cutlery industry, Sheffield was changing from a rural market town to a smoky manufacturing center when this picture was drawn by E. Blore and engraved by George Cooke.

86. KNIFE BLADES, late 1700s. These butcher-knife blades bear the "Cross and L" mark, first registered in Sheffield, England, in 1750. Made to be attached to handmade wood or bone handles by the rivets visible in the tangs, these blades (8-3/4" by 1-1/8" and 8-1/2" by 1") were found with others in a rock crevice near the Witch Tree on Hat Point, east of Grand Portage Bay. They are corroded from exposure.

87. *THE EUROPEAN FACTORIES, CANTON,* 1843. China was both a source for trade goods like vermilion and a market for furs. In this engraving by J. Tingle from a sketch by Thomas Allom, ships crowd the harbor of Canton in front of the establishments of European merchants.

88. VERMILION, late 1700s? Vermilion (mercury sulphide) was produced in China and shipped to England before coming to America. The pigment could be rubbed into skin, wood, bone, or hides, or mixed with water or grease for face and body paint. In the late 1700s and early 1800s it was shipped inland in leather bags and kegs; later it was packaged in paper. This remnant of a bulk shipment (3-1/4" by 2-1/2" by 1-1/2") was found in the Granite River by the Quetico-Superior Underwater Research Project. See color page 61.

89. *VIEW OF MURANO, THE SEAT OF GLASS MANU-FACTURE,* 1880. Most beads traded to American Indians were produced on the island of Murano in Venice, shown here in a 19th-century engraving.

90. VENETIAN BEADS, mid-1800s. Venice, Italy, was the center of the beadmaking industry during the fur trade, though other cities competed. Polychrome "fancy" beads like these (1/4" to 1-1/8" long), hand-decorated in contrasting colors of glass, were particularly likely to be made in Venice. This type of bead is often found in far western archaeological sites dating to the middle or late 1800s.

Not every fur was sold to an Indian middleman before coming to a European trader. A beaver might also be caught by a hunter from a band living near the post. Such bands lived a somewhat different life from their neighbors farther away. They provided services that kept the trade running smoothly. Men hunted for meat; women harvested crops and cured pelts. These people might earn a living in the fur trade without trapping furs at all.

JOURNEY OF A FUR
COMING TO THE POST

91. *INDIANS CARRYING FOOD*, c.1870. Robert O. Sweeny, a St. Paul druggist and illustrator, drew this pencil-and-ink sketch on paper.

THE HAND THAT FEEDS YOU

A fur trader's canoe often set out from the east only two-thirds full of trade goods—the rest was provisions. Even so, the supply of food was seldom enough to last out the journey to the trading post. Throughout the winter, the trader relied on the Indians for food.

Great Lakes Indians had gotten food from agriculture for many centuries before traders came. But instead of plowing up large fields for crops like the Europeans, Indians harvested a variety of foods that grew wild in abundance. Bands living near a post had a market for their wild rice, maple sugar, and corn, and traders sold them metal tools for digging their gardens, parching wild rice, and boiling maple sap. European tools also made fishing and hunting easier. The surplus of food created by these new technologies supported the movement west of European traders.

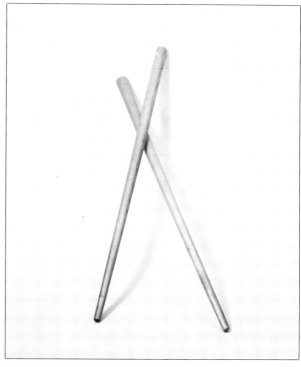

92. GATHERING WILD RICE, 1853. Women knock ripe kernels into their canoe in this engraving by James Smillie from a watercolor by Seth Eastman.

93. WINNOWING BASKET, early 1900s. Wild rice was parched, pounded, and winnowed to remove the husks before storage. This tray (18-1/8" long by 17-7/8" wide by 4-3/4" deep) of birch bark stitched with spruce root to a wooden rim is part of a set collected from Ojibway residents of Grand Portage by ethnologist Frances Densmore in 1930.

94. RICING STICKS, early 1900s. Wild rice was one of the main exports of the St. Croix River Valley and of northern Minnesota during the 18th and early 19th centuries. Sticks like these were used to knock the ripe rice kernels off the stalks and into canoes. Ojibway people at Grand Portage created these sticks (25" long) for ethnologist Frances Densmore in 1930.

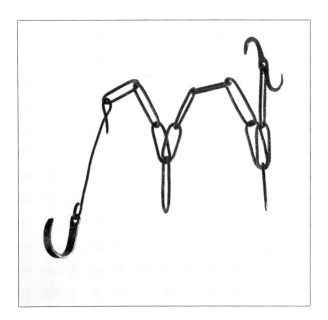

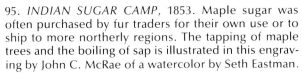

95. *INDIAN SUGAR CAMP*, 1853. Maple sugar was often purchased by fur traders for their own use or to ship to more northerly regions. The tapping of maple trees and the boiling of sap is illustrated in this engraving by John C. McRae of a watercolor by Seth Eastman.

96. COPPER KETTLE, undated. Kettles revolutionized maple sugar processing, as they could be hung directly over a fire. Kettles like this one (7" diameter by 6-1/8" high) are shown being used for gathering and boiling down sap in illustrations by Seth Eastman. Lacking its lid, it was acquired in the Lac La Croix area. The wire bail wraps around projecting lugs of handwrought iron. The Hudson's Bay Company introduced such kettles in about 1780 and sold them into the 1900s.

97. CHAIN FOR A MAPLE SUGARING KETTLE, late 1800s? Maple sugar was boiled into a thick syrup in large kettles suspended over open fires by chains. This hand-forged iron chain (50-1/2" long) was found in 1961, buried with an old brass kettle at a sugaring site by Sugarbush Lake in the Grand Portage Indian Reservation. Its links are 3-1/8" to 4-3/4" long.

98. SUGARING PADDLE AND TROUGH, undated. Hot maple sap, poured into a trough, was stirred with a paddle until it crystallized. This paddle (43-1/4" by 2-7/8"), allegedly 150 years old, once belonged to George Big Bear of the Ojibway community at White Earth. The trough (27" by 13-3/4" by 6-1/8") is from Waconia.

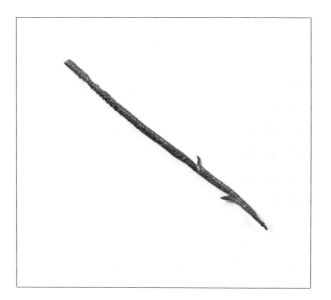

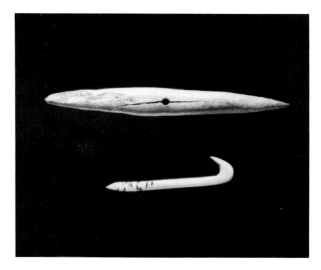

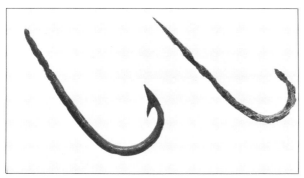

99. *SPEARING FISH IN WINTER*, 1853. The use of spears for killing fish is shown in this engraving by Charles E. Wagstaff and Joseph Andrews from a watercolor by Seth Eastman.

100. FISHHOOKS, 1704–1776. Hooks of iron wire were attached to the line with a variety of knots or hitches. These two corroded hooks were excavated at Fort Senneville on Montreal Island, Ottawa River, a French site occupied from 1704 to 1776. They probably once had flattened portions at the ends for attaching a line. Lent by Royal Ontario Museum, Toronto.

101. FISH SPEAR, late 1700s? This spear (5" long) of round steel wire may have been used, mounted on a long wooden handle, to catch small fish or frogs. Its tang end has horizontal grooves to keep it firmly seated in the handle socket. Barbed on opposite sides of the shaft, it was excavated at the North West Company depot, Grand Portage, in 1963.

102. BONE FISHING EQUIPMENT, 1700s? Indians continued making bone fishing tools even after metal goods were available. One tool (top, 3-1/4") may be a gorge hook for large fish or a needle for weaving nets. It was recovered at Fort St. Charles on Lake of the Woods (1732–1750s). The carved bone fishhook (1-3/4") is from Mandan villages along the Missouri and Heart rivers, N.Dak., occupied from the mid-1600s to the late 1700s.

103. FISHNET FLOATS, early 1900s. Fish were a year-round source of food for both hunters and traders. Fishnets of imported twine were set under the ice in winter and in open water in summer. These Ojibway wooden floats (14" to 18-1/2" long) collected by ethnologist Frances Densmore are similar to those used centuries ago.

104. IRON HOE, undated. Iron hoes were much in demand by Indian farmers at least as early as the 1760s. Hand-forged in a method similar to axes, the blade of this example (7-3/4" long by 5-1/2" across blade) bears swirling patterns from the manufacturing process. Found within the North West Company stockade, Grand Portage, it may have been made by a post or reservation blacksmith.

105. *GUARDING THE CORN FIELDS,* 1853. The people living south of the Great Lakes raised corn for sale to traders as well as for their own use. One Ottawa village at L'Arbre Croche, Mich., planted large fields to supply the post at Michilimackinac. This engraving by James Smillie from a watercolor by Seth Eastman shows a field of corn tended by Dakota women, probably near Fort Snelling.

106. MORTAR AND PESTLE, undated. Corn kernels were usually parched over a fire and pounded into meal with a mortar and pestle. This pestle (42-1/8" long by 5-1/2" diameter), carved of a single piece of wood, is a Plains Indian piece collected by anthropologist Gilbert L. Wilson in the early 1900s. The mortar (19" by 8-1/4") was made from a hollowed-out log.

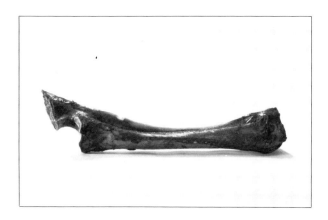

CURING

Furs were highly perishable. Maggots, mold, and moths might attack the pelt as soon as it was removed from the carcass. So before its long journey to Europe, the fur had to be cleaned and dried. The first step in processing furs was done by Indian women, whose skills and labor were valuable commodities with which they could buy what they needed.

If the fur was to remain on the pelt, the woman washed it to remove blood and dirt. Next she scraped excess flesh and fat from the inside of the skin with a flesher. The last step—drying and stretching—varied with the type of fur and its intended use. Beaver, mink, fisher, and muskrat each had its own kind of stretching frame. Once they dried, the pelts were stiff and hard as boards.

Hides used for clothing or moccasins needed more: Soaking, removing the hair, scraping off the flesh, oiling with brains, stretching, breaking the grain, and smoking might take several days.

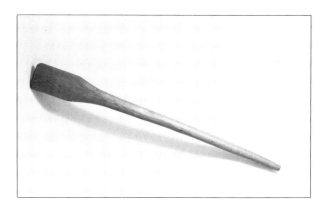

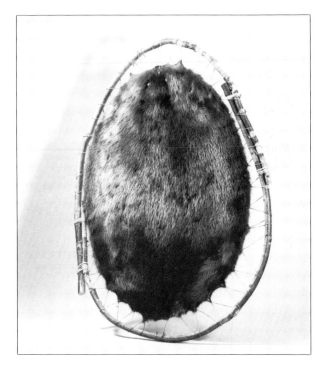

107. SCRAPER, early 1900s. This tool for removing hair from skins was made from the hind leg bone of a moose. Hides to be used for clothing, rope, or moccasins were soaked and laid out on a log, then scraped clean with a bone or iron tool. Ethnologist Frances Densmore bought this specimen (19" long) in 1930 from the Grand Portage Ojibway woman who made and used it.

108. TANNING PADDLE, early 1900s. The Ojibway of northern Minnesota used wooden paddles to rub and stretch skins in one of the last steps of the curing process. Ethnologist Frances Densmore collected this specimen (33" by 2-3/4") from the Grand Portage Ojibway.

109. STRETCHED BEAVER SKIN. Beaver skins were nearly circular, so they were dried and stretched on hoops of willow. This modern example shows the method of lacing the skin onto the hoop with sinew. Courtesy Old Fort William, Thunder Bay, Ontario.

110. *INDIANS PREPARING HIDES*, c.1860. This ink-wash-and-pencil sketch on paper by Robert O. Sweeny shows three steps in the process of curing hides. A woman smokes a skin (left), another cleans the flesh off the back (center), and another sews a skin into the desired shape.

111. STRETCHER FRAMES, early 1900s. For centuries trappers have used cedar boards to stretch and dry the skins of small animals. The skin was turned inside out and slipped over the board to dry. These boards (24-1/4" by 5-1/2" to 13-3/8" by 1-3/4") collected near Crane Lake were probably used (left to right) for fisher, marten, muskrat, and mink.

112. TOOLS FOR CURING HIDES, late 1700s? These tools had separate uses in processing hides. The bone tool (bottom, 8-5/8" long) has a sharp-toothed edge for removing flesh from the inside of a skin. The L-shaped antler scraper (top, 13-1/4" by 6-1/8") was for removing hair. A sharp stone or metal blade was inserted in the notched end and secured by rawhide thongs. Both were collected by archaeologist Jacob V. Brower near Mandan, N.Dak.

After its long journey across the sea, the ax arrived at Montreal, where goods were bought by traders preparing for their voyage to the west. But before he could leave Montreal, each trader had to satisfy government regulations.

Through its history, the fur trade was closely controlled by the governments of France, Britain, or America. To limit the number of traders and control their activ-ities, law required licenses for anyone going into Indian country.

A licensed trader usually stayed in the west and trusted his agent in Montreal to send supplies. The agent stored the axes and other goods until spring, then re-packed them all in compact, watertight *pièces* (bales, kegs, or cases) weighing about 90 pounds each. He then entrusted them to a crew of hired canoemen.

JOURNEY OF AN AX
COMING TO THE POST

113. *MONTREAL*, 1842. The bustling harbor of Montreal is shown in this lithograph based on a painting by Coke Smyth. John Carter Brown Library, Brown University, Providence, R.I.

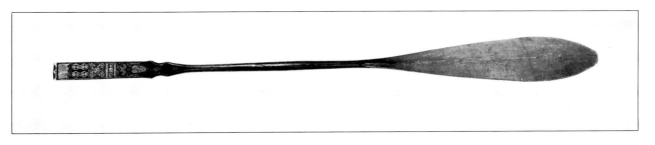

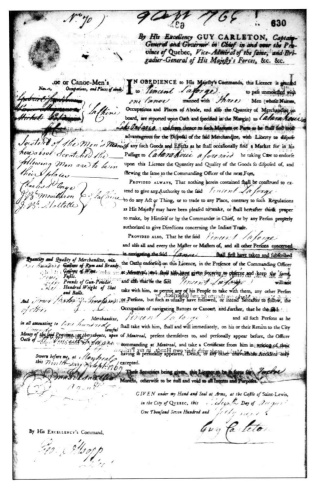

SINBADS OF THE WILDERNESS

After leaving Montreal, the ax entered one of the most elaborate inland water transportation systems in the world—one depending almost entirely on canoes. So great was the distance and so expensive the labor of paddling and portaging, that the ax might double or triple in value by the time it reached the far end of the Great Lakes.

The men who provided this labor were called *voyageurs*—the French name for travelers. They were the manual laborers of the fur trade. Like transportation workers everywhere, the voyageurs developed a language, dress, and folklore of their own. Those who worked on the Great Lakes were called *mangeurs de lard* (pork-eaters). These men were novices compared to the *hivernants* (winterers) who took the freight to inland posts and spent the winter with the Indians. The expertise of all these low-paid workers kept the fur trade going in spite of frequent changes in government and company ownership. The men who got rich in the fur trade were always changing; the men who stayed poor in the fur trade were always the same.

114. VOYAGEUR PADDLE, undated. This carved wooden paddle (76-1/2" by 6-3/8") resembles the shape of paddles used by some eastern tribes. The initials "WD" appear on the ornately carved handle of the stained and varnished artifact, which shows no signs of use. It was allegedly lost in an Indian battle on the St. Croix River. Some speculate that this was the 1839 Dakota attack on an Ojibway party at Stillwater involving a trading party under William Aitken.

115. TRADING LICENSE, 1769. Vincent Laforge obtained this trading license from Guy Carleton, British governor of Quebec. In exchange, he posted bond and promised to comply with regulations and uphold the authority of King George III. This is the first of four pages, which also listed his canoemen and merchandise. Laforge had to have his license endorsed in Montreal and again swear allegiance to the king. Public Archives of Canada.

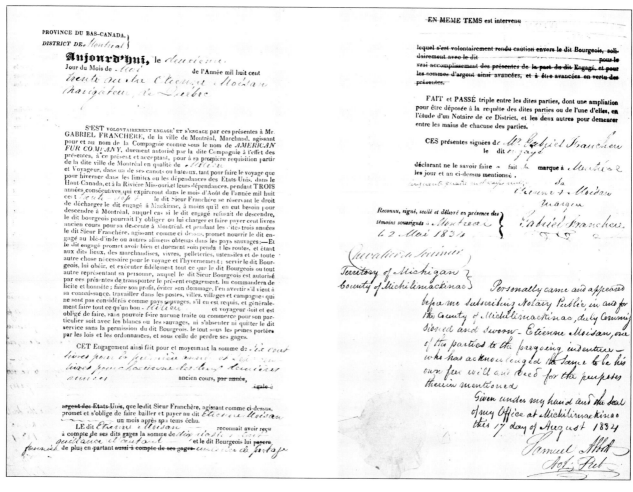

116. *CANOT DE MAITRE*, 1822. John Halkett of the Hudson's Bay Company made this watercolor of a 36-foot Montreal canoe manned by 14 voyageurs and carrying two passengers. Hudson's Bay Company. See color page 71.

117. VOYAGEUR ENGAGEMENT, 1834. In this three-year contract with Gabriel Franchere, representative of the American Fur Company, Quebec navigator Etienne Moisan promised to serve his employer as a mid-man and voyageur in return for 600 pounds the first year and 700 pounds each of the two following years.

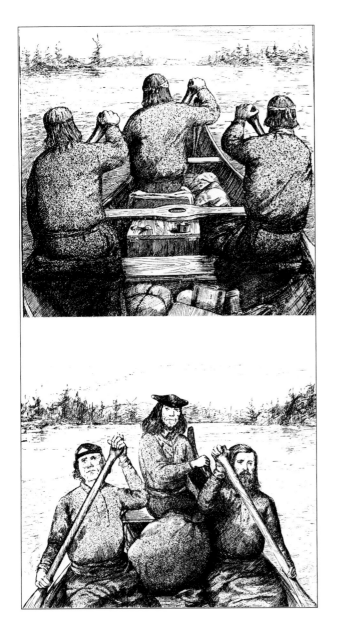

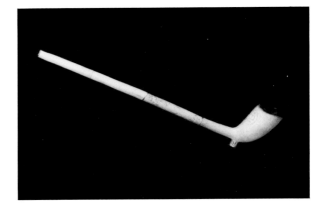

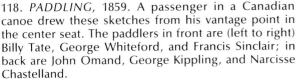

118. *PADDLING*, 1859. A passenger in a Canadian canoe drew these sketches from his vantage point in the center seat. The paddlers in front are (left to right) Billy Tate, George Whiteford, and Francis Sinclair; in back are John Omand, George Kippling, and Narcisse Chastelland.

See color page 69:
119. SASH, undated. Colorful woolen sashes made at the town of L'Assomption, northeast of Montreal, became the trademark of voyageurs in the early 1800s, but they were also traded to Indians. The technique of finger weaving was borrowed from Indians living nearby. Two parallel strips of cloth are pieced down the middle of this example, forming a zigzag pattern.

120. CLAY PIPE, late 1700s. A voyageur's work was measured with his pipe; periods of work were punctuated by regular rests for smoking, and the distance covered between rests came to be called a *pipe*. This English white clay pipe (9-1/8" long), a disposable item used by all social classes, was excavated at Grand Portage in 1963. Its bowl, marked "TD," was found separately from the stem. It has been smoked.

121. SASH, early 1800s? The lightning-bolt pattern gives this *ceinture flechée* or arrow sash its name. Finger-woven of white, dark and light blue, red, yellow, and green wool, it is typical of sashes made at L'Assomption, Quebec. It was woven from the center out and has braided fringes (29-1/2" long). The Codere family of Montreal owned it for at least three generations before giving it to the MHS. It measures 88-1/8" by 6-1/2".

A trader's post was more than just a store: It was home, foreign embassy, and local tavern, too. Here people of two worlds met and exchanged their wealth and values.

In the far north, most posts were large, permanent structures built with the idea that the Indians would travel there only once a year for trade. But in the Great Lakes area, traders sought out Indian bands rather than waiting for the Indians to come to them. Their posts were small, temporary buildings, often abandoned after a year or two of use. Such a "wintering" post was occupied from about September to May, and most of the trading was done in the fall and spring. Through the winter, while the gentleman in charge looked after the post, his voyageurs made frequent trips *(derouines)* out to visit and trade with Indian families in their hunting territories.

THE TRADING POST

122. *AMERICAN FUR CO*. *BUILDINGS, FOND DU LAC. (BACK VIEW),* 1827. A sketch by Thomas L. McKenney of the United States Indian Department probably was the source of this engraving from his book, *Sketches of a Tour to the Lakes.* The post was at present-day Duluth.

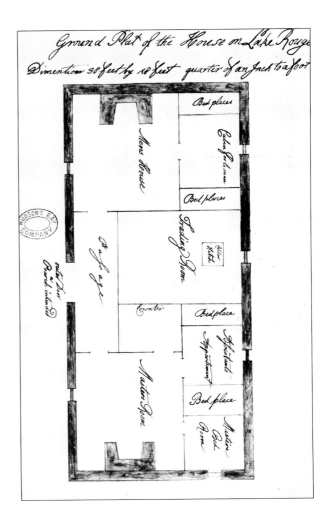

123. *FUR TRADERS AT YELLOW LAKE, WISCONSIN,* 1856–1860. Franz Hölzlhuber did this watercolor while visiting a fur post at Yellow Lake, Wis. Photographed by Ron Marsh, Glenbow Museum, Calgary, Alberta.

124. *WITH THE FUR TRADERS ON YELLOW LAKE,* 1856–1860. Shelves of cloth bolts for sale in a post at Yellow Lake are pictured in this watercolor by Franz Hölzlhuber. Photographed by Ron Marsh, Glenbow Museum, Calgary, Alberta.

125. *GROUND PLAT OF THE HOUSE ON LAKE ROUGE,* 1790. This manuscript floor plan of a trading post built by James Sutherland of the Hudson's Bay Company at Red Lake, Ontario, shows that trading post architecture strictly segregated the gentlemen from the voyageurs.

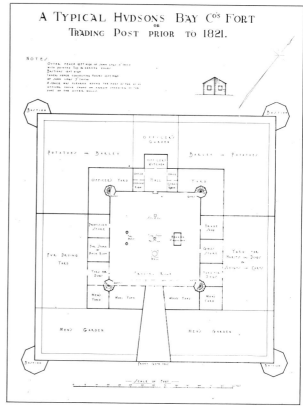

126. *INTERIOR OF THE HUDSON BAY CO. POST AT PEMBINA ON THE RED RIVER,* c.1847. This pen-and-ink sketch by Hampton Moody shows a small post on the Canadian border. C-35062/Public Archives Canada.

127. *A TYPICAL HUDSONS BAY CO'S FORT OR TRADING POST,* c.1887. This idealized plan of the permanent establishments of the Hudson's Bay Company prior to 1821 shows their intended self-sufficiency. Hudson's Bay Company.

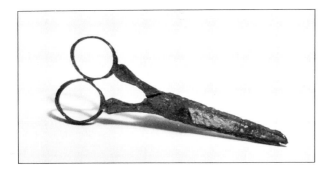

KEEPING UP APPEARANCES

European traders took much of their world into the wilderness. Clothing, customs, and possessions all helped keep cultural ties and memories strong. Belongings were also the outward symbols of class distinctions, very important in a trading post. At the top of the scale was the *bourgeois*, or regional manager of a string of posts. Next in line was the *commis*, or clerk, who might manage a single post. At the bottom was the illiterate *voyageur*, who was like an indentured servant.

Men in the fur trade had to know their place. The gentleman in charge could bring a *cassette* (chest) of his own belongings. The fur companies outfitted voyageurs with only two blankets, two pairs of trousers, two shirts, and some tobacco each. Gentlemen had their own stores of tea, coffee, chocolate, and brandy. Voyageurs drank water and rum. Gentlemen ate off china. Voyageurs ate from kettles. The importance of class symbols brought luxuries like pewter and bone china to posts in the wilderness.

128. SCISSORS, late 1700s? These light sewing scissors (4-3/4" long by 1-5/8" wide) excavated at a warehouse site outside the North West Company's stockade at Grand Portage are an example of personal belongings from the post. There was once a shell design on the handles at the base of the rings.

129. BUCKLES, late 1700s. These common articles of clothing were excavated at Grand Portage in 1963. The plain iron buckle (left, 1-1/2" by 1") used for belts, packsacks, and other straps was found at a warehouse site outside the North West Company palisade. The decorated brass buckle (right, 1-5/8" by 1-3/8") was probably used by a gentleman to fasten breeches at the knee. The cross bar and fastening prongs are missing.

130. DINING UTENSILS, 1751–1805. A pewter teaspoon (left, 5-1/4" long) from the North West Company kitchen fireplace at Grand Portage sports a dotted border on its handle. It probably dates 1787–1805. The touchmark on the pewter spoon (middle, 7-3/4" long) found by the Quetico-Superior Underwater Research Project in the Granite River identifies it as the work of James Boost of London (fl. 1751–1767). A "crowned X" Pewterers' Company mark shows the metal's high quality. The iron fork (right, 8-1/8" long) from the North West Company depot, Grand Portage, is fastened to a bone handle by three rivets.

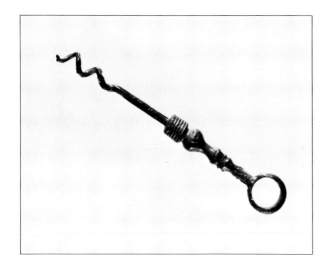

131. CORKSCREW, late 1700s. The corked bottles that this iron utensil was used for opening were probably reserved for use by gentlemen; liquor for voyageurs came in kegs. Found at Grand Portage in 1964, the artifact (4" long) has a finely turned handle. A sheath covered the point when not in use and was inserted through the loop for leverage when pulling a cork.

132. TEAKETTLE, late 1700s? This copper kettle may have been the property of a clerk or *bourgeois*, to whom the luxuries of tea, coffee, and chocolate were available. The kettle (8" maximum diameter by 5-1/2" high), recovered by the Quetico-Superior Underwater Research Project in rapids between Gunflint and Little Gunflint lakes in 1960, is missing its cover and handle. See color page 63.

133. METAL BUTTONS, 1750–1812. These buttons once adorned the clothing of Grand Portage traders and employees. They are made of silver, brass, copper, silver- and gold-plated brass and copper, and German silver. Eight are cast buttons with spun backs and brass wire eyes set into a boss on the button back; three have brass eyes soldered to the button back; and two are cast as one piece. Their diameters are 1-1/8" to 1/2".

134. SHOE BUCKLE FRAMES, late 1700s. For fashionable frontiersmen, shoe buckles were a necessity until they went out of style in the 1790s. These buckles were probably the property of gentlemen. The cast brass buckle (left, 4" by 2-1/2") was found in the Granite River. The silver-plated iron buckle (top right, 3-7/8" by 2-1/4") and the brass buckle (bottom right, 4-1/8" by 2-1/4") were found at Grand Portage.

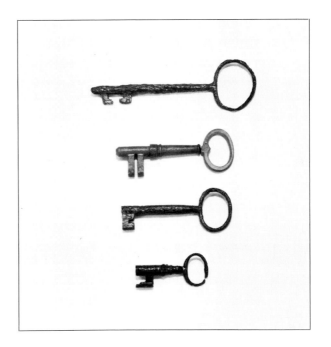

PRIVATE PROPERTY

A trading post was like a giant lock protecting the merchandise brought with such trouble from distant parts of the world. A trader had to keep careful track of inventory, and a trading post was laden with locks, hooks, and fasteners to keep goods in and people out.

The European system of commerce was based on the idea of private property. In a trading post, doors and shutters divided space into private rooms, where belongings were fastened inside chests and trunks. In contrast, in an Ojibway wigwam, most goods and spaces were shared. A man was expected to share with all his relatives. A host and guest shared all they owned with each other. A well-to-do person shared his food with someone less fortunate. Some traders saw the Indian system and began to wonder whether "property of Goods [was not] the only source of all the Disorders that perplex the European Societies."

135. SPIGOT AND VALVE COLLARS, late 1700s. Rum and brandy were carefully dispensed from wooden kegs with brass spigots. For security, some spigots had collars so they could be opened only with a specially shaped key. This spigot (5-1/4" long by 1-5/8" high) has a fluted, tapered back end that fits into the bung hole of a barrel; the front end has a platform for hammering it in. Both spigot and collars (1" by 1") were found at the North West Company kitchen at Grand Portage.

136. KEYS, early 1800s? Keys excavated at the North West Company depot at Grand Portage in 1963 include (top to bottom) an iron door key (5-1/8" long), a matching bronze shank and ring (3-5/8" total) found separately, an iron door or padlock key (3-1/4"), and an iron key (2-1/8") for a trunk or cupboard.

137. PADLOCKS, late 1700s–early 1800s. These handcrafted padlocks are of iron or steel. One (upper left, 3-1/2" high by 2-1/2" wide by 3/8" thick) is from the Big Sandy Lake fur post used by the North West and American Fur companies between 1794 and 1832. Its keyhole cover plate has stamped initials. The two small locks with a black lacquer finish (upper right, 2-1/8" by 1-3/4" by 1/2"; lower left, 2-3/8" by 1-3/4" by 1/2") and the large lock with attached wire (4-1/4" by 3-1/2" by 1-1/4") were found in kitchen and warehouse sites at Grand Portage.

[My] men finished the Store & put all the provisions & Goods under Lock & Key, a happy Circumstance in time of Danger.
— John Sayer, fur trader, 1804

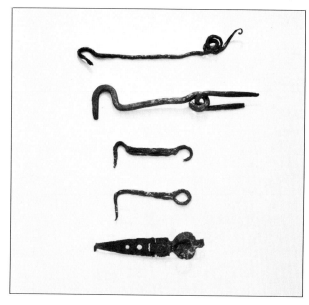

138. LOCK PARTS, late 1700s. Standard lock mechanisms were imported for use in posts. Top to bottom are a latch mechanism found at the North West Company depot, Grand Portage, of a size (8-3/4" by 5/8") used in a door lock; a complete lock (5-7/8" by 3-1/2") with a smaller version of the same mechanism still in place, recovered from the Sandy Lake post; three lightweight iron locks found at Grand Portage, of the size (4-1/8" by 2-3/4", 4-3/4" by 3", and 3-3/4" by 2-1/4") used in chests, cupboards, or trunks.

139. DOOR HANDLE AND LATCH, late 1700s. This iron door handle (10-1/2" high by 6-1/8" wide) excavated at Grand Portage in 1937 has a simple thumb latch. Forged from round bar stock, it was fastened to the door with two nails or screws.

140. KEYHOLE ESCUTCHEONS, early 1800s? These metal plates are all that remain of their keyholes. One (left, 1-3/4" by 1") was handmade from a brass kettle scrap and found at Grand Portage. The large, heavy brass escutcheon (right, 2" by 1-1/4") was excavated at Big Sandy Lake. It is marked "W & E Jacot / Birmingham." Its provenance is uncertain.

141. HOOKS AND HINGED HASP, late 1700s. Securing devices used at Grand Portage include (top to bottom) a hook of round iron wire (6-3/4" long) possibly used for fastening shutters open; a door hook (4-5/8" long excluding staple) still attached to a staple for fastening to a wooden door; two cabinet or door hooks (3-1/8" and 3" long) made from flat iron stock; and a hasp (4-1/8" long) used with a padlock for securing a desk or chest.

BARGAINING

Fashion reigned here as imperiously as in more civilised lands; some fine, richly-coloured, oval beads, the size of pigeon's eggs, which I considered my best . . . were despised and out of date, while the little trashy white ones, no bigger than a pin's head, were highly appreciated. . . . The small beads were valued . . . for embroidery . . . while the larger ones . . . had come to be thought too barbaric.
—James Carnegie at Fort Carlton, 1859

142. *THE TRADING-STORE,* 1848. A Canadian trading post in the far north is shown in this engraving from Robert M. Ballantyne's *Hudson Bay; Or, Everyday Life In the Wilds of North America.*

I did my best to secure 10 Beaver skins that [Pichiquequi] has in his lodge. I gave him a small Tin Basin that he Asked for, to make himself a pipe. I proposed to trade them for Rum, for merchandise, silverware, Beads, all in vain, he was absolutely unwilling to give [the skins] to me . . . replying that he loved them. I offered him a blanket to no avail. He [said] that he was Keeping them to make a robe . . . to Cover him in The night.
—Michel Curot, 1804

143. *INDIANS BARTERING,* 1842. This lithograph based on an oil painting by Coke Smyth shows a bargaining session. John Carter Brown Library, Brown University, Providence, R.I.

You told me Last year to bring many Indians, you see I have not Lyd here is a great many young men come with me, use them Kindly! . . . Tell your servants to fill the measure and not to put their fingers within the Brim . . . give us good black tobacco, moist & hard twisted. Let us see itt before op'n'd. . . . The Guns are bad, Let us trade Light guns small in the hand, and well shap'd, with Locks that will not freeze in the winter, and Red gun cases. . . . Let the young men have Roll tobacco cheap, Kettles thick high for the shape, and size, strong Ears, and the Baile to Lap Just upon the side,—Give us Good measure, in cloth,—Let us see the old measure, Do you mind me!
—Cree chief to a trader, 1743

144. *CAPTAIN BULGER, GOVERNOR OF ASSINIBOIA, AND THE CHIEFS & WARRIORS OF THE CHIPPEWA TRIBE, OF RED LAKE, IN COUNCIL,* c. 1823. This watercolor by Peter Rindisbacher shows negotiations between an official of the Hudson's Bay Company–sponsored Selkirk settlement and a Chippewa delegation at the Colony House, Fort Douglas, Winnipeg, May 22, 1823. Hudson's Bay Company Collection; lent by W. A. Bulger.

We cannot omit to accquaint you of the Deceit of the Smiths who take our Money & instead of putting Steel into our Hatchets put Iron, so that as soon as we come into our Country to use them they fall to pieces.   —an Iroquois spokesman, 1701

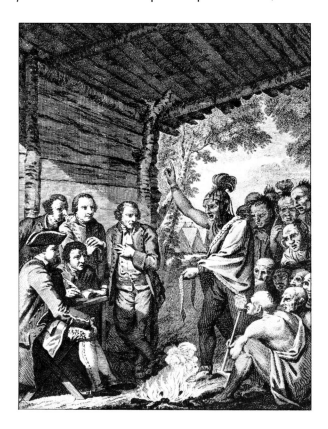

145. *THE INDIANS GIVING A TALK TO COLONEL BOUQUET,* 1766. An Indian orator holding a wampum belt addresses a British officer in this engraving of an event in Pontiac's War, from an original by Benjamin West.

PAYING

Beaver skins were a cumbersome currency; so some fur companies issued paper money and coins. But mostly they carried on the fur trade by credit. People quickly found that debt established ties of mutual dependence between traders and customers.

Once he had advanced goods, the trader knew that his customer probably would not take furs elsewhere. Since the debtor's family could also pay in food or services, a trader's life was more secure.

Debt also gave the Indians power over the trader. If a hunter died from hunger, he would never pay. So the trader was committed to his welfare. But best of all, debt made traders more dependable. As long as Indians owed him, the trader could not afford to leave their village. So Indians used small debts to keep traders they liked and large ones to get rid of those they didn't like.

146. NORTH WEST COMPANY TOKEN, 1820. Clearly used as an ornament as well as a medium of exchange, this token was struck in Birmingham by John Walker & Company, and was probably worth one beaver skin. The North West Company seems to have distributed these coins mostly in the Columbia River Valley region of Oregon. Lent by Oregon Historical Society, Portland.

147. CURRENCY, early 1800s. This paper currency, issued by the American Fur Company's Northern Outfit prior to 1842, was probably meant not for paying Indians for furs, but for circulation among company employees and dependents in the large trade-based métis community at La Pointe, Wis. This two-note lithographed sheet (6-1/4" high by 7-1/8" wide) is blank on the back.

148. TRADING TOKENS, c.1854. These four brass tokens were issued by the Hudson's Bay Company for the use of employees and customers at the Eastmain post on James Bay. They are worth 1/8, 1/4, 1/2, and one "made beaver," a unit of currency equal to one prime beaver pelt, by which post accounts were kept. Lent by Royal Ontario Museum, Toronto.

149. INKWELL, late 1700s. Portable writing utensils were essential for keeping records in a highly mobile business. This copper- or brass-clad glass inkwell (1-1/2" high by 1" diameter) excavated at Grand Portage could fit into a portable desk or a pocket. Threaded for a screw-on top, it would have been used with a quill pen.

150. LEDGER PAGE, 1831. American Fur Company trader Alexis Bailly, operating a post at Mendota, recorded the transactions of one customer on each page of his ledger. The left column shows debits for purchases; the right, credits for furs brought in. The standard of currency is the muskrat skin.

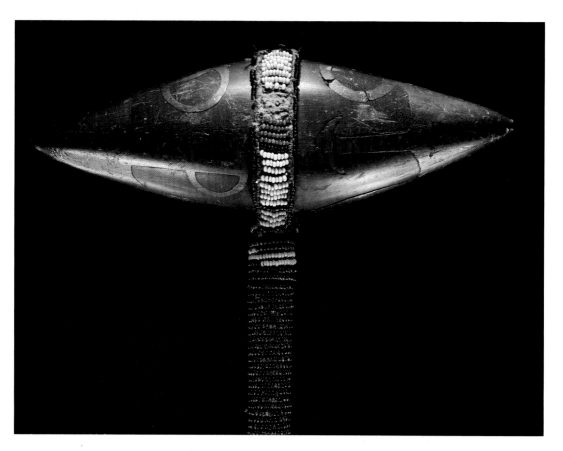

191. CEREMONIAL CLUB, undated. See page 91.
  2. BIRCH-BARK BOX, late 1800s? See page 6.   220. SILVER CROSS, 1767–1809. See page 100.

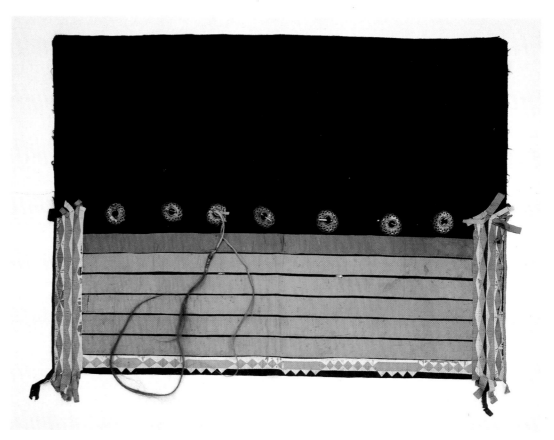

43. EFFIGY PIPE, undated. See page 18.
233. BLANKET WITH RIBBON APPLIQUE, pre-1863. See page 105.

234. YARN BAG, early 1900s. See page 106.
 88. VERMILION, late 1700s? See page 33.

232. MIRROR, undated. See page 104.

224. PIPE TOMAHAWK, c.1860. See page 101.
132. TEAKETTLE, late 1700s? See page 50.

162. BRITISH FLAG, c.1815. See page 77.

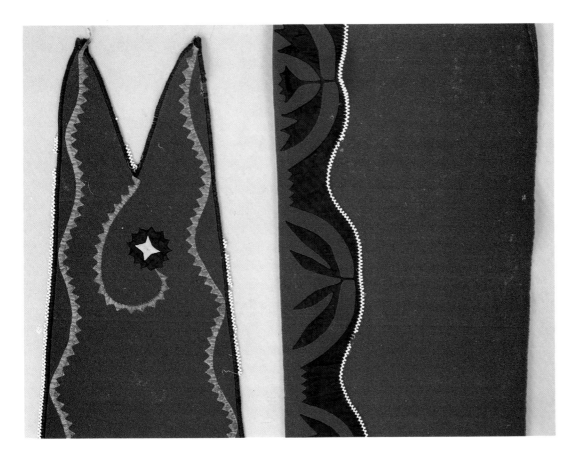

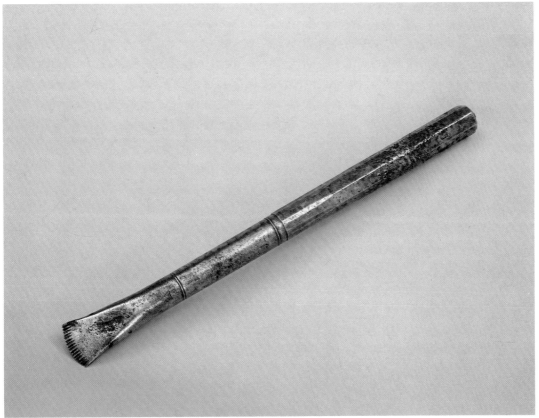

212. SASH, mid-1800s? See page 97.
186. HIDE FLESHER MADE FROM A GUN BARREL, mid-1800s. See page 89.

30. GLASS BEADS, late 1700s. See page 14.

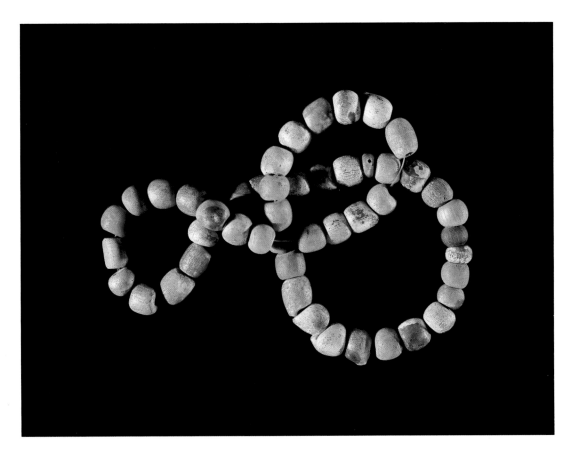

20. GLASS BEADS, early 1600s. See page 11.
40. GLASS BEADS, mid-1800s. See page 17.

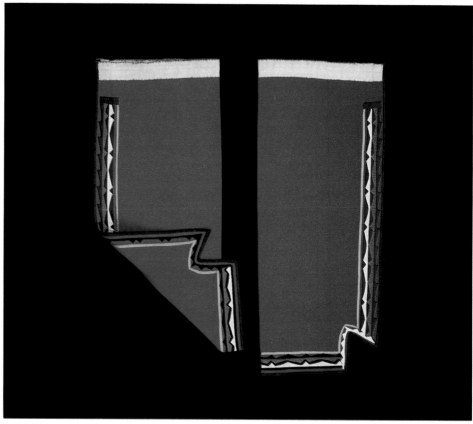

207. WOOLEN SHIRT, undated. See page 96.
208. WOOLEN LEGGINGS, undated. See page 96.

119. SASH, undated. See page 45.

54. *LA CACCIA DEI CASTORI,* 1760. See page 20.

70

116. *CANOT DE MAITRE,* 1822. See page 44.

57. *CANADIAN INDIANS SPEARING BEAVER,* 1830–1834. See page 22.

OJIBWE INDIANS AT GRAND PORTAGE, 1857. Trade blankets, cloth, and silver were part of the lives of these women painted in oil by Eastman Johnson. St. Louis County Historical Society, Duluth.

PRICES

What was the ax worth? To the trader it was worth the number of furs that paid for its manufacture, transportation, insurance, and taxes—plus a little left over for profit.

What was the fur worth? To the Indian it was worth as many trade goods as made hunting and curing worthwhile.

Traders' costs varied from year to year and place to place, but the usefulness of an ax stayed the same. Since the trader valued the ax in terms of profit and the Indian valued it in terms of usefulness, they often disagreed on the price. When the price was assigned, a strange transformation took place. The beaver, which had been an animal, became a unit of currency. The prices of all the trader's goods were figured according to a unit of value equal to one good beaver skin. And the hunter's labor was counted in beavers, not in hours.

These price lists are based on the records of François Victor Malhiot, who traded for the North West Company on the south side of Lake Superior in 1804.

151. PRICE LIST. Art by Earl Gutnik.

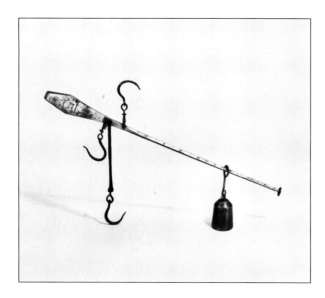

KEEPING TRACK OF THE BUSINESS

A trader's success depended upon making a profit. To know where he stood, he had to have information about his stock, his customers, and his competition.

Europeans invented many devices to measure what they were selling. Cloth and ribbon sold by the yard (*verge*), shot by the pound (*livre*), and liquor by the pint (*chopine*). The trader's clerks compiled pages of records accounting for all the goods and furs.

But no measuring device could tell the trader about his customers and competition. For that he relied on his friends in the Indian bands. They brought news on the state of hunting, on the prices, quality, and quantity of his competitors' goods, and on the whereabouts of parties with furs.

152. STEELYARD, 1850. Storekeepers and traders measured goods sold by weight on handwrought steelyards like this example (19-7/8" long) that weighs articles from 1 to 45 pounds. From Cooperstown, N.Y., the steelyard was made by J. P. Shumway of Ashford, Conn. It was probably never used in a fur post.

153. INVENTORY OF GOODS, 1830. Alexis Bailly made an inventory of the goods he supplied to Joseph R. Brown, a subsidiary trader. Both worked for the American Fur Company, Bailly at Mendota and Brown among the Dakota at Lake Pepin.

154. SHOT MEASURES, late 1800s? These standard-sized metal cups were used to measure portions of shot at the Hudson's Bay Company post on Albany Island, Ontario, possibly as late as the 1900s. Lent by Royal Ontario Museum, Toronto.

155. INVENTORY OF FURS, 1830. The packs of furs shipped east for the American Fur Company by Alexis Bailly's outfit at Mendota are listed in this inventory.

Trade . . . is the chief Cement which binds us together. —Peter Wraxall, British Indian Secretary for New York, 1754

Commerce is the great engine by which we are to coerce them, and not war.
    —Thomas Jefferson, 1808

POLITICS

A fur trading transaction meant more than does an exchange at a modern department store. Among Great Lakes Indians, an exchange of goods was an exchange of friendship or political alliance. Soon the Europeans, bargaining hard for the alliance of powerful tribes like the Huron, Iroquois, Dakota, and Ojibway, adapted to gift-giving customs. At solemn ceremonies they bestowed medals, flags, and uniforms upon leaders who might aid them in commerce and war.

But ordinary trade goods that changed hands every day conferred on Europeans a far more lasting economic power.

156. *CAPTAIN W. ANDREW BULGER SAYING FAREWELL AT FORT MCKAY,* c.1823. Indian allies were often the deciding factor in struggles between European powers in America. A British commander bids farewell to Indian allies after capturing a fort at Prairie du Chien, Wis., in the War of 1812, in this pen-and-watercolor sketch by Peter Rindisbacher. The incident took place in 1815. Amon Carter Museum, Fort Worth.

157. PEACE MEDAL, 1814. European powers presented medals to Indian leaders to encourage political alliance. This silver medal (3" diameter) showing a bust of King George III of England was used to repair British-Indian alliances during the War of 1812. It was passed down in a Grand Portage Ojibway family until 1979. The reverse side bears the royal coat of arms.

158. PEACE MEDAL, 1801. The United States bargained for power in the West with medals like this one given to a prominent Dakota leader, probably Tatankamani or Red Wing. Found in 1871 by street graders in Red Wing, the medal (4-1/8" diameter) is the largest Jefferson medal cast, indicating a recipient of some importance. The two sides are separate sheets of silver united by a rim.

159. PEACE MEDAL, 1853. This silver Franklin Pierce medal (3" diameter) probably commemorated an Ojibway chief's participation in 1855 negotiations at Washington, D.C., to cede Ojibway lands in northern Minnesota Territory. The obverse side shows President Pierce and is inscribed "Presented to the Chippewa Chieftain Hole-in-the-day." In 1893 William P. Clough purchased the medal from William F. Campbell, who may have obtained it from Hole-in-the-Day's widow.

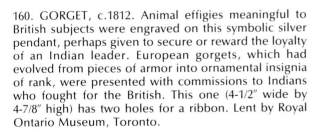

160. GORGET, c.1812. Animal effigies meaningful to British subjects were engraved on this symbolic silver pendant, perhaps given to secure or reward the loyalty of an Indian leader. European gorgets, which had evolved from pieces of armor into ornamental insignia of rank, were presented with commissions to Indians who fought for the British. This one (4-1/2″ wide by 4-7/8″ high) has two holes for a ribbon. Lent by Royal Ontario Museum, Toronto.

161. CERTIFICATE OF RECOGNITION, 1816. Commissions were often given with medals to Indian leaders. William Clark, governor of Missouri Territory, testified to Tah-mah-hah's loyalty in the War of 1812 with this certificate. It appointed Tah-mah-hah a Dakota chief, though his band recognized Red Wing or Tatankamani. This is one of two copies Tah-mah-hah had made.

162. BRITISH FLAG, c.1815. This flag was a symbol of alliance presented by British officials to an Ojibway leader. It was passed down in a Grand Portage Ojibway family until 1979. Its Red Ensign design (a Union Jack on a red field) is of the type flown by British navy and merchant ships after 1801. Measuring 51-1/2″ by 94-1/2″, it is hand-stitched out of six loosely woven woolen strips. See color page 64.

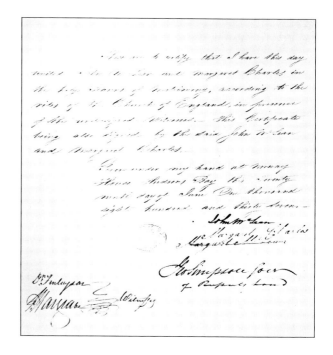

FAMILY

To both Europeans and Indians, marriage was a way of making important alliances. European merchants relied on their families for financial, political, and other support. Indians saw kinship as a system that defined a person's allegiance in war, diplomacy, and trade. When a European married an Indian woman, both family networks merged to become the trader's insurance, law court, news agency, trade partners, and police.

Many sorts of marriages were formed between European traders and Indian women. Some were frankly political, for a trader could gain prestige and influence by forming ties with a powerful Indian family. Other traders married to gain a translator of foreign language and customs, or a worker to make canoes, snowshoes, and moccasins.

Eventually, marriages performed "in the fashion of the country" (according to Indian rites) became accepted by Europeans. The mixed-blood children of these unions often entered the fur trade themselves. With ties to both worlds, they formed the nucleus of a tight-knit fur trade community.

163. MARRIAGE CONTRACT, 1837. In the absence of churches and courts, the Hudson's Bay Company legitimized the marriages of its employees to Indian and métis women. John McLean and Margaret Charles signed this contract at Norway House on Lake Winnipeg. Hudson's Bay Company Archives, Provincial Archives of Manitoba (B.154/2/1 fo 421).

164. *INDIAN WOMEN IN TENT*, c.1830. Peter Rindisbacher painted this watercolor of an Indian or métis family gathered inside a tepee. West Point Museum Collections, United States Military Academy.

165. *PORTRAIT OF A BOY*, 1857. This charcoal drawing was one in a series of sketches of Ojibway family life executed by Eastman Johnson at Grand Portage. St. Louis County Historical Society, Duluth.

166. *PORTRAIT OF A GIRL*, 1856–1857. This charcoal drawing was one of a series of sketches of Ojibway family life executed by Eastman Johnson at Grand Portage. St. Louis County Historical Society, Duluth.

WOULD YOU MARRY THIS MAN?

Advantages
- He might come to live with your family, so they would never lack for trade goods.
- If trade was good, you and your husband might have power throughout the Lake Superior region.
- You would be rich, so none of your family would starve.

Disadvantages
- He might want you to leave your family and live among strangers.
- He might decide to leave you and move back east.
- He might want to marry a white woman later and say you are not legally his wife.
- He might want to raise your children as Europeans and send them away to school.
- He might want you to change your ways and beliefs and act like a European.

In 1792 O-shaw-gus-co-day-way-quah was living with her family on the south shore of Lake Superior when a young Irish trader named John Johnston asked for her hand in marriage. This was not surprising, for the young woman's father was the powerful Ojibway leader, Waubojeeg. Any trader who could ally himself to Waubojeeg by marriage would have a great advantage in trade with the Lake Superior bands.

But the trader Johnston was new to the area, and no one knew his reputation. So Waubojeeg told the young man to return to Montreal that summer, and if he still wished to marry an Indian woman the next year, to come back and ask again. When Johnston returned the next year, Waubojeeg, impressed by the young man's sincerity, told his daughter that she would be the trader's wife.

O-shaw-gus-co-day-way-quah refused, but her father would hear none of it. She was married to Johnston against her will. He took her away from her family to live at Sault Ste. Marie (now in Michigan). There she grew accustomed to her new life and fond of her husband. They were happily married for 36 years and had eight children. He was a successful trader; she became one of the most powerful women in the Lake Superior region.

167. *JOHN JOHNSTON*, 1789. This oil painting by James Wilson shows John Johnston three years before he met O-shaw-gus-co-day-way-quah. Bayliss Public Library, Sault Ste. Marie, Mich.

168. *SUSAN JOHNSTON*, 1826. This oil painting attributed to Charles Bird King shows O-shaw-gus-co-day-way-quah in later life. Buffalo and Erie County Historical Society, Buffalo, N.Y.

When all the bargaining was done, the ax and the fur changed hands. The fur was shipped back to Europe to be made into hats or trimming for fashionable garments. The ax became an Indian tool for chopping firewood, making canoes, and catching more beaver.

The ax and the fur ended their long journeys by reinforcing foreign values and ways of life. The ax became one of many tools that took part in a flowering of traditional Indian culture. The beaver hat became a symbol of the European class system.

In Europe, the fur was graded and sold with others at a great auction in London, or Paris, or Moscow. Many were re-exported to other lands, particularly to China.

In the hands of European artisans, the furs were transformed into luxuries for the rich. Furriers used the fine furs of fox, sable, and ermine to trim coats and make mittens and muffs. Deerskins were sold for leather. The beaver and muskrat were reserved for making fine felt hats. Fashionable shops advertised the exotic origins of their wares.

JOURNEY OF A FUR
IN EUROPE

169. *FOURREUR*, mid-1700s. This engraving from Denis Diderot's *Encyclopédie* shows a Paris furrier's shop with muff-lined walls and pelts hung from the rafters. A man, right, beats the insects out of a fur.

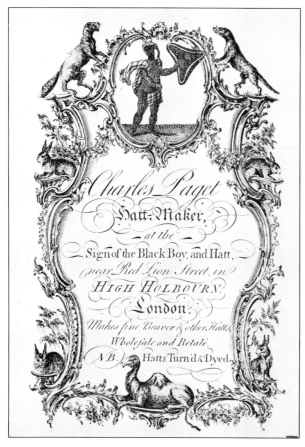

170. THE WELLINGTON. This style of beaver hat was popular around 1812.

171. TRADE CARD, c.1760. London hatmaker Charles Paget used exotic animals including a camel to advertise his tricorn hats.

172. MAN WITH A MUFF, 1779. Fine furs were used for trimming clothes and for accessories like muffs, worn by both men and women. Large muffs like the one in this French fashion plate were worn on a ribbon around the neck.

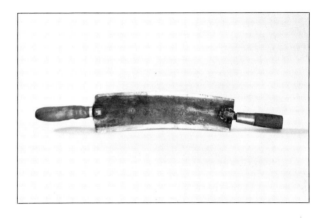

THE HATTER'S ART

Most beaver furs were used in the making of felt hats. Beaver was particularly suited to this process because the microscopic barbs on the hairs cling together, forming a strong felt mat.

Only one part of the beaver pelt was used for making hats: the soft, fine undercoat. First the long guard hairs on top were plucked away; then the underfur was shaved from the skin. A pile of loose fur was mixed by the vibrating string of a hatter's bow, then shaped and pressed into a bat. Repeated boiling and pressing shrank and thickened the felt. Fitted over a hat-shaped block, it was pressed and steamed into the proper shape. Final brushing gave the beaver hat a fine, glossy surface.

173. A HATTER MAKING FELT, mid-1700s. Once the fur was shaved from the pelt, it was placed on a specially designed table or *hurl* and mixed by the vibrating string of a hatter's bow. This caused the microscopic barbs on the beaver hairs to catch together, forming a strong felt bat. This engraving is from Diderot's *Encyclopédie*.

174. FURRIER'S KNIFE, 1911–1965. Tools of the tanner and furrier changed very little from the 18th to the 20th centuries. This shaving knife (23-1/2" by 3-1/2"), nearly identical to 18th-century ones, was used for cleaning flesh and hair off furs before making felt and leather. Stamped "W.H. Horn & Bro.," it was used by John M. Thill, who worked for St. Paul furriers Joseph Ullman, Inc., and the Rose Brothers Fur Company.

175. HAT BLOCK, late 1800s. Hat blocks were used for shaping and ironing both beaver and silk hats. On each side of this block is a removable wooden piece making it easy to fit a man's tapered top hat onto the block (8" high by 8-1/2" diameter). With the hat snugly secured, the device could be attached to a lathe for ironing. Donors Adolph and Lillian Hartman probably used this hat block in their Minneapolis millinery shop.

A. To take off your hat properly, first stand gracefully facing the person you wish to honor.

176. PAYING RESPECTS, 1725. These engravings and instructions are from Pierre Rameau's guide book on etiquette and manners, *The Dancing Master*.

PAYING RESPECTS

The beaver felt hat was a symbol of social class. A man wore a hat in the presence of someone of higher status only when invited to do so. To refuse to remove your hat was an act of protest. The precise way of doffing the hat expressed subtle shades of deference.

_____

Among the actions of the greatest import—the doffing of the cap takes first place, as being the action devised by men to do honour and reverence to one another. —Marco Caroso

The Savages have very little regard for the Rules of Civility in use among the Europeans; nay, they even fall a-laughing, when they see our People employ'd in paying mutual respects one to another. —Louis Hennepin, 1698

B. Raise your right arm to the height of your shoulder, keeping your hand open. Never use your left arm to take off your hat.

C. Bend your elbow in a graceful semicircle toward your hat. Place your thumb against the side of your forehead and lay four fingers upon the brim of your hat. Never let your arm hide your face.

D. Pick up the hat and follow steps A and B in reverse. Hold the hat at your side so that the inside points forward and the crown points back.

E. Place your left foot a little forward, keeping your weight on your right leg. Bend your right knee a little.

F. Bow from the waist. Bow your head as well, but always look at the person you are saluting.

G. Shift your weight onto your left leg and rise. Put your hat on the same way you took it off. Never press your hand on the hat's crown to make it fit snugly.

The tools brought by the fur trade to America did not at once change the Indians' lives. This was because they did not buy things alien to their way of life. Pocket watches, padlocks, and shoe buckles were of no use to a hunter or his wife. Instead, the Indians took things that did the same jobs as tools they already had, only better.

In their new owners' hands, many trade goods were transformed into things that served different needs than the trader had foreseen. They became Indian, not European, tools. And yet the trade goods were profoundly foreign. They came not from the forest, but from outside. Their prices were not measured in hours of work, but in abstract values. They were products not of the intimate ties between humans and other creatures, but of ties with markets, commerce, and profits. The Indians were not their creators, but their consumers. The artifacts on the following pages show how trade goods were adopted into Indian life.

JOURNEY OF AN AX
IN AMERICA

177. *A MAN & HIS WIFE RETURNING WITH A LOAD OF PARTRIDGES FROM THEIR TENT,* c.1805. In this watercolor, métis artist William Richards recorded how trade goods were adopted into a new way of life by Indians at James Bay. Hudson's Bay Company Archives.

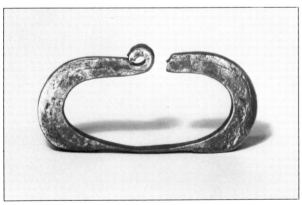

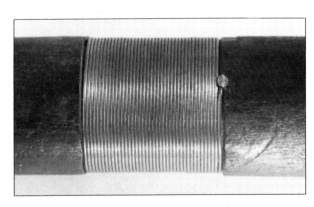

178. SCRAPER MADE FROM A CERAMIC SHARD, late 1800s. Plains Indians transformed a broken porcelain dish into this tool for scraping hides. The shard (2-3/4" by 2-1/2") is a piece of ordinary whiteware probably dating from 1860 to 1890. Anthropologist Gilbert L. Wilson, who worked with the Hidatsa, collected it.

179. FIRE STEEL, mid-1800s. The striking edge of this fire steel (3-1/2" by 1-1/2") has been worn away. Used by Pillager Ojibway Chief Flat Mouth (either Eshkebugecoshe or his son Niganibines) in 1854, it was donated by Indian agent Charles H. Beaulieu, member of a fur trading family that lived for many years with the Ojibway at Crow Wing, Leech Lake, and White Earth Reservation. Beaulieu's father Clement was the elder Flat Mouth's interpreter at an 1855 treaty signing.

180. CATLINITE ORNAMENT MOLD, early 1800s? A local craftsman created this mold (5-7/8" by 4") to replicate trade silver ornaments. The slab of pipestone, found buried in St. Paul in 1857, was probably first used for other purposes, as it has faintly scratched animal glyphs on the surface. The patterns, which have sprue holes for the entry of molten metal into the mold, are mostly standard late 18th century European shapes.

181. WIRE-WOUND PIPESTEM, undated. Indians used snare wire for more than trapping. This stained wooden pipestem (32" long) was wrapped in wire at regular intervals for decoration. Two gauges of wire, copper and brass, were used. Early pipes were sometimes similarly wrapped with porcupine quills.

182. WIRE-WOUND PIPESTEM, undated. Detail of above.

183. STONE AND METAL PIPE BOWLS, 1867 and undated. New materials like metals were quickly transformed into traditional shapes by Indian craftsmen. A traditional Ojibway-style steatite pipe (top, 5-1/4" long by 3" high by 3/4" wide) made at Leech Lake in 1867 is almost perfectly reproduced in the white metal pipe (bottom, 3-3/4" long by 2-1/4" high by 5/8" wide), which features incised lines around the bowl rim, a prow-shaped projection on the front, a ridge along the base, and vertical lines where the wooden stem attaches to the bowl. This well-made metal pipe bowl was plowed up near Pokegama Lake, probably in the late 1800s. Lead pipe bowls resembling it are not uncommon.

184. WAR CLUB, undated. A handle shaped like a European weapon earns this Indian piece the name "gunstock club." First recorded in the 1600s, such clubs were used until after 1850. Collected among the Ojibway at White Earth Reservation, the club has a metal spearhead (5-3/4" long), brass tacks on both sides of a stained wooden haft (29"), and a file-burned grip.

185. POWDER FLASK AND ORNAMENT CUT FROM FLASK, mid-1800s? Metal powder flasks, though introduced late to the trade, were promptly transformed. This ornament (right, 3-1/8" by 2-1/8"), cut from a flask and pierced for suspension, was excavated at Grand Portage. Its design is typical of Birmingham manufacturers, c.1825–1890. Compare it with the uncut flask (7-3/8" by 4-1/8"), similar to those made by George and J. W. Hawksley of Sheffield, c.1845–1889.

GUN BARRELS
Old gun barrels were retired because they were apt to explode. To extend their useful life, Indians shaped the barrels into fleshers, scrapers, and chisel handles.

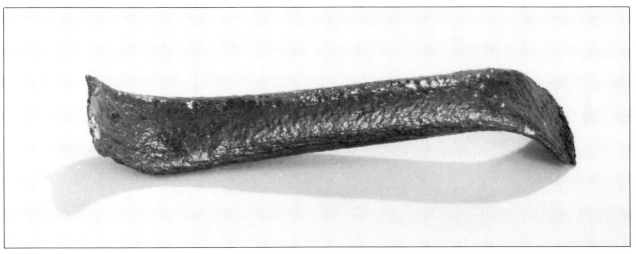

186. HIDE FLESHER MADE FROM A GUN BARREL, mid-1800s. An Indian workman sawed off the breech end of a gun barrel, flattened one end, and filed teeth into the flat edge to make this tool (15" long) for fleshing hides. The barrel, from one of the cheap Belgian rifles imported by American traders after about 1830, is stamped with a spurious Birmingham proof mark and a "tombstone fox" symbol to pass it off as British. See color page 65.

187. FLESHER MADE FROM A GUN BARREL, late 1700s? This handcrafted iron or steel scraper (7" long) probably was made from the barrel of a fowling piece. Bent into an S-shape with flattened ends, it may have been used as a flesher for scraping hides or as a quill flattener. It was excavated in the North West Company kitchen area at Grand Portage.

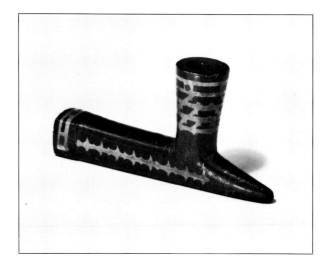

LEAD

Great quantities of lead were brought into North America in the form of musket balls, shot, unworked blocks, and bale seals. The availability of this soft metal gave rise to the new art form of lead inlay. Soon Indians were mining their own lead in Illinois.

188. MUSKET BALLS, late 1700s. Musket balls not only were used as ammunition, but also were melted down for raw lead by Great Lakes Indians. These examples (1/2″ diameter) were among 1,066 balls found by the Quetico-Superior Underwater Research Project at Basswood River. They were cast in molds and are often irregular in shape.

189. PIPE BOWL, 1800s? This Ojibway pipe bowl (5-1/8″ long by 2-1/2″ high) is made of steatite, lead inlay, and chips of pipestone. Willard B. Heath, a schoolteacher on the Red Lake Reservation from 1881 to 1884, collected it at Red Lake.

190. PIPE BOWL, late 1800s? The geometrical designs on this steatite pipe bowl (6-1/8″ long by 3-1/8″ high) were executed in pewter. The Ojibway pipe is from the White Earth Reservation.

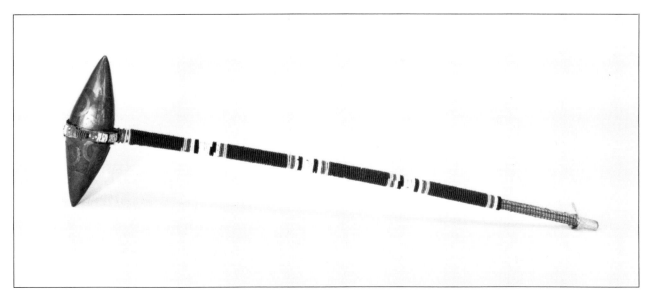

191. CEREMONIAL CLUB, undated. The head of this club is made of pipestone mined by Indians in southern Minnesota. To make the lead inlay, a design was carved into the stone; then the head was wrapped tightly in leather or bark. Molten lead was poured into the carved channels. When the lead cooled and the wrapping was removed, the metal was filed flush with the stone. The club (24-1/2" long by 6-3/4" across head) is of Dakota design. See detail color page 58.

192. FISHNET SINKER, late 1800s? This handcrafted cylinder (3-3/8" long) pounded from a lead sheet still had fishnet twine inside it when excavated at Grand Portage in 1963. The American Fur Company carried on an extensive fishing operation at this post in the late 1830s; the sinker may date to or postdate that era.

193. ALTERED LEAD SEALS, 1700s. Lead seals were broken when removed from bales. The one at center (2-3/4"), marked "IHI" or "THI," was discarded and later excavated at Grand Portage. Sometimes seals were recycled. One (left, 1-1/8"), from Grand Portage, has an arrowhead outline on its back, possibly scratched as a pattern for cutting. Its front is marked "McT," possibly for the McTavish supply firm of Montreal. Another item (right, 1-1/8") made from a broken seal or flattened musket ball, from Fort St. Charles, resembles an 18th-century toy called a *whizzer*, except that it has one hole instead of two.

FILES

Files were essential for sharpening knives and axes, creating metal arrowheads, and repairing the metal parts of guns. Heated, they were used to burn designs on wood. Worn, they were transformed into spearheads, fire steels, and chisels.

194. FIRE STEEL MADE FROM A FILE, undated. Someone meticulously reforged a file into this fire steel (4" by 1-5/8"), similar in shape to steels sold by English trading companies. Anthropologist Gilbert L. Wilson collected this item in North Dakota in the early 1900s.

195. FILES, 1774–1802. These new files were bound for a trading post. Instead they ended up at the bottom of Big Parisien Rapids on the French River, Ontario, and were recovered by divers for the Royal Ontario Museum in 1962. The two on top (9-7/8" by 3/4" and 8-3/4" by 3/4") are rectangular cross-section, double-cut files; at bottom is a half-round file (9-7/8" by 7/8") with a crown mark and the letters "CA" on its tang.

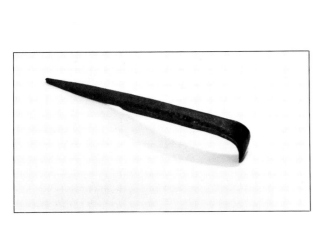

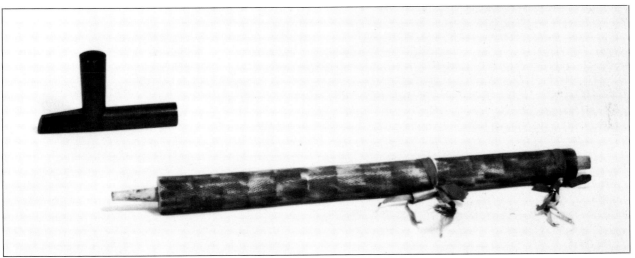

196. FLESHER MADE FROM A FILE, undated. The owner of this file (9-1/2″ by 1-1/2″) heated and hammered the end into a curve, transforming it into a tool for scraping the flesh off the inside of a hide. Ethnologist Frances Densmore collected it at Grand Portage in 1930.

197. FILE-BURNED PIPESTEM, late 1800s. Worn files could be used as decorating tools. This pipestem's crosshatch pattern was burned in with a heated file. A Dakota piece (18-3/4″ by 1-1/4″ diameter) decorated with ribbons, hair, and tinkling cones, it was collected along with a matching bowl before 1919, probably near the town of Pipestone.

198. CHISEL MADE FROM A FILE, undated. This chisel found around 1900 by archaeologist Jacob V. Brower at Mille Lacs Lake, was made from a file by sharpening one end into a blade. The tip of the tang at the other end of the artifact (11-1/8″ by 1-1/2″) has been flattened by striking.

KETTLES

Kettles were used not just for cooking and fetching water. They were the Indians' primary source of sheet copper and brass. An old kettle's rim could be sheared off and the remainder used to create spearheads, patches for other kettles, ornaments, and knives. A favorite use of kettle metal was for tinkling cones, hung on clothes or pouches to make a jingling sound.

199. PATCHED KETTLE, late 1800s. Old kettle metal was frequently used for patching other kettles like this one. Patched in a number of places with metal scraps and homemade rivets, this brass artifact (10″ high by 15-3/4″ maximum diameter) was collected by Harry D. Ayer in the Ojibway community at Mille Lacs Lake.

200. BRASS ORNAMENTAL DISCS, undated. Large flat discs of shell, stone, or copper were worn as chest ornaments by tribes south of the Great Lakes long before trade goods became available. Identical to prehistoric examples, these discs (5-3/4″ and 4-3/4″ diameters) are of brass, probably cut from a kettle. Most likely attached to clothing by thongs, or worn at the neck, they were excavated in the late 1800s in Hamilton County, Tenn.

201. SCRAPS OF KETTLES, late 1700s. These scraps are from kettles cut apart for the metal. Both the sheared-off copper kettle rim (13″ maximum diameter) and the L-shaped copper scrap (10-1/8″ by 9-3/4″) with punched holes and folded rim were excavated at the British Fort Charlotte.

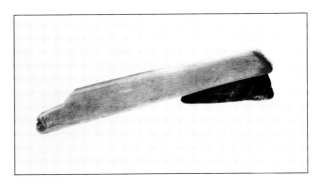

202. POUCH WITH TINKLING CONES, late 1800s? Tinkling cones fringe this hard leather pouch, identified by the donor as a mirror case (5" by 3-1/4"). Beside it lie detached cones (3/4" to 1-3/4") decorated with red-dyed animal hair, woolen cloth, beads, and feathers. One is from Grand Portage. Colonel Haydn S. Cole, who served in the United States Army 1885–1892 during the Plains Wars, collected the white, red, and blue beaded case, decorated with a Chinese coin.

203. PROJECTILE POINTS OF KETTLE METAL, 1700s. These two handmade artifacts were fashioned from kettles. One (left, 3" long) was excavated at Grand Portage in 1963 and may date to the late 18th or early 19th century. The other (right, 1-1/2" long) was recovered at Fort St. Charles, a French site dating from 1732 to the 1750s.

204. KNIFE MADE FROM A KETTLE SCRAP, late 1700s? This knife (5-7/8" by 1-3/8") was made by inserting a sharpened copper kettle scrap into a deer rib. Archaeologist Jacob V. Brower found it during excavations of Mandan Indian trash heaps (dated prior to 1800) near the Heart River, N.Dak., in the late 19th century.

205. SCRAPS CUT FROM KETTLE METAL, various dates. These brass and copper cuttings include (top to bottom) eight diamond-shaped pieces possibly meant for janglers, excavated at Grand Portage; four restrung cylindrical beads excavated at Mandan Indian sites near the mouth of the Heart River, N.Dak.; and heart-shaped and octagonal pieces found at Grand Portage in 1963. All measure less than 2" across. Some may be kettle patches or scraps left over from cutting other shapes.

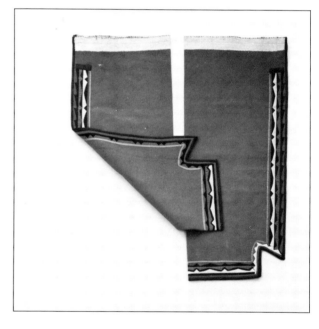

CLOTH

Cloth was imported in many forms: in bolts, blankets, ribbons, braids, and finished into shirts, coats, and trousers. Cloth was better for clothing than skins because it was lightweight, easier to sew, colorful, and washable. It quickly became the most important fur trade item. In 1786, for example, one trader named Jean Baptiste Cadotte received a yearly shipment of goods, with 55 percent of its value in cloth.

The Indians did not always use cloth in its original form. They made blankets into hooded coats *(capotes)* or unraveled them for the yarn. Ribbon, available in huge supply after the French Revolution spurred a simpler style of dress in Europe, was adopted by Indian women for appliqué.

206. WOOLEN HOOD, early 1900s. Northern tribes frequently made pointed hoods from traders' blankets. This one, made by Grand Portage Ojibway and collected by ethnologist Frances Densmore in 1930, is of gray wool decorated with yellow and black fringe. Gathered at the back of the neck and tying under the chin, the hood (17-1/4" high by 11-3/4" wide) resembles those in 19th-century paintings of Indian life.

207. WOOLEN SHIRT, undated. This shirt (31-1/8" long by 23-5/8" wide at the hem) may have been made from a blanket or cloth bought from a trader. Its deep V-shaped neck is surrounded with floral embroidery and blue silk ribbon. The cuffs have white glass buttons. It was donated with the red wool leggings. See color page 68.

208. WOOLEN LEGGINGS, undated. Ready-made leggings and shirts were often sold by traders, but this example seems to have been constructed by Indian people. The leggings (26-5/8" long by 11" wide) of red wool are decorated with silk ribbon appliqué differing in design on the two sides. They were donated with the red wool shirt. See color page 68.

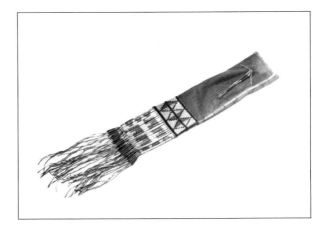

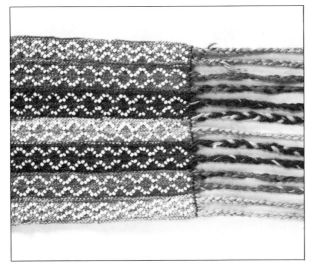

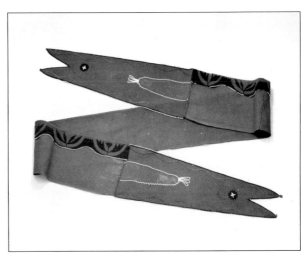

209. CLOTH BELT, undated. One side of this belt (41-3/8" by 2-3/8") is of dark green wool edged with white seed beads stitched in the "vertical-horizontal" pattern. The other side is lined with a gold, green, brown, and black floral cotton print, and the edges are bound with red cloth tape. On the ends are hide thongs and tassles.

210. WOVEN SASH, mid-1800s? Great Lakes Indians made finger-woven sashes long before they had European goods, but the art flourished with a ready supply of trade yarn. White seed beads are woven directly into this Ojibway sash (22" long by 4" wide with 21" fringes) from Crow Wing. Seven narrow strips of green, red, blue, and yellow yarn form the body of the sash. It is said to have been owned by Ojibway leader Hole-in-the-Day (1828–1868).

211. PIPE BAG, late 1800s. This Plains Indian bag (34-5/8" by 5-1/2") is identical in design to earlier examples, but made of red wool rather than hide and decorated with beads and metal tinkling cones in addition to the traditional porcupine quills. The bag may be made from a recycled trade blanket.

212. SASH, mid-1800s? This sash was pieced together from four sections of red wool, with blue, green, and cream silk ribbons appliquéd in stylized floral patterns. In the main body of the sash, the ribbon is sewn onto a flap edged with seed beeds. The sash (104-1/2" long by 7-3/4" wide), said to have belonged to Hole-in-the-Day (1828–1868), is from Crow Wing. See detail color page 65.

The fur that came to Europe was a messenger of great changes on the way. Like a stone dropped into a quiet pool, trade with America spread widening circles of change through European culture. Tastes, manufacturing, technology, and ideas all felt the influence of contact with American Indians.

The astonishing discovery of people living by customs and morals wholly foreign immediately set European philosophers debating. Were the Indians savages whose lives were "solitary, poor, nasty, brutish, and short" or were they the ideal of uncorrupted humanity living in harmony with natural laws? When traders and travelers brought back accounts of Indian ideas about property, marriage, and government, some Europeans wondered whether these ideas were not more pure and unspoiled than their own.

I am as free as nature first made man,
Ere the base laws of servitude began,
When wild in woods the noble savage ran.
　　　　　　　　　—John Dryden, 1670

JOURNEY OF A FUR

THE TRADE OF IDEAS

213. *REYSE DOOR NIEUWE ONDEKTE LANDEN*, 1698. To some Europeans, Indians symbolized uncorrupted humanity living in harmony with natural law. This detail of an engraving from a Louis Hennepin travel narrative shows an imaginary Indian lord, dispensing a cornucopia of natural resources.

TEXTBOOKS OF TRADE

Few Europeans observed Indian culture more carefully than the traders whose livelihood depended on it. In their continual effort to "discerne what sorte of Goods goes best," traders observed the Indians' tastes, habits, and values. The information they sent back was transformed into new sorts of merchandise. In the end, traders found themselves stocking goods that had no parallel in European culture.

214. SPOON LOCKET, undated. Canadian silversmiths produced lockets of this shape in the late 1700s and early 1800s. Earning its name from its concave shape, the bowl (2-1/2" by 1-7/8") was not necessarily made from a spoon. The flat lid (2-3/4" by 2") was originally hinged and probably latched with a hasp protruding through the slot. Engraved with a wavy feathered line and maker's mark "JM" or "IM," it was found at Cedar Lake in Crow Wing County near an 1806 North West Company post site.

215. REAL AND IMITATION WAMPUM, undated. When Europeans discovered that beads carved from conch and clam shells (wampum) were prized by inland tribes, they began to make the white-and-purple beads for sale. Even easier to make were glass imitations. One string (top, beads 1/8" long) is real shell wampum from New York. The other (bottom, beads 1/4" long) is glass, found in the Basswood River.

216. GLASS BEADS AND DENTALIUM SHELLS, undated. Dentalia from the Pacific Coast (right, 5/8" to 1-1/8" long) were traded to Great Lakes Indians for use in necklaces and embroidery. Archaeologist Jacob V. Brower recovered these at Mille Lacs Lake in the late 1800s. Traders introduced nearly identical decorative material (left, 1-1/8") in these white tubular beads, probably also from Mille Lacs.

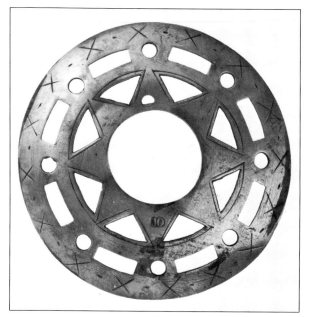

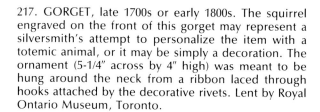

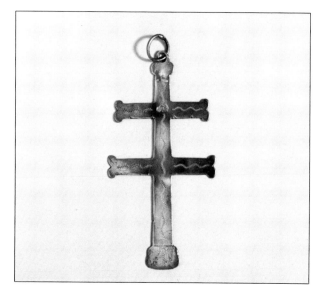

217. GORGET, late 1700s or early 1800s. The squirrel engraved on the front of this gorget may represent a silversmith's attempt to personalize the item with a totemic animal, or it may be simply a decoration. The ornament (5-1/4" across by 4" high) was meant to be hung around the neck from a ribbon laced through hooks attached by the decorative rivets. Lent by Royal Ontario Museum, Toronto.

218. BROOCH, late 1700s or early 1800s. Convex brooches like this one were mass-produced out of thin sheet silver and worn in profusion on the clothing and in the hair of Great Lakes Indians. This example (2-1/2" diameter) lacks its pin. Its maker's mark is "JO," possibly for Montreal silversmith John Oakes (fl. 1780–1814). Lent by Royal Ontario Museum, Toronto.

219. SILVER ARMBAND, undated. This armband (1/2" wide) of thin sheet silver has a bent tab on one end that fits into a slot on the other. Stamped along the upper edge is a scalloped pattern. The band (2-1/4" diameter) apparently has been cut from a larger piece, as fragments of another pattern are visible along the lower edge. It was excavated near Birmingham, Ala., probably in the late 1800s.

220. SILVER CROSS, 1767–1809. Silver ornaments, a major trade item in the late 1700s, were made mostly in Philadelphia, Albany, Montreal, and Quebec. This double-barred cross by Montreal silversmith Robert Cruickshank was found in Wisconsin around 1830. The cross (3-1/4" by 1-1/8") was sold as a decorative rather than as a religious piece. See color page 59.

100

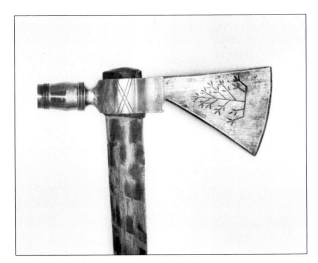

221. BEAVER PENDANT, late 1700s. Silversmiths and pewterers soon learned to copy the totemic art of their Indian customers—not necessarily because they understood its symbolism but because such wares sold quickly. This molded white metal beaver (1-3/4″ by 3/4″) mimics effigies long carved from pipestone by Great Lakes Indians. Its maker's mark is "DW" or "DVV."

222. HAIR PLATE, mid-1800s? The style of silver brooches worn in the hair by Great Lakes Indians was elaborated by Plains Indians into long strings of graduated discs, both homemade and supplied by traders catering to changing fashions. This set of 12 nickel silver hair plates, purchased from photographer Truman W. Ingersoll in 1889, is mounted on a tapered hide backing (14-3/4″ long). A cluster of feathers and three twisted rawhide strands decorate the top.

223. PIPE TOMAHAWK, c.1860–1880. This iron- or steel-headed weapon, which appears to have been smoked, is typical of those traded to Plains Indians. It has a diamond-shaped eye and a barrel-shaped bowl. The blade (9-3/4″ long) has a hole surrounded by stamped rays. Brass tacks and ribbon decorate the ash haft (21-3/4″). Alonzo P. Connolly, who fought in the Dakota War of 1862, collected the Dakota artifact.

224. PIPE TOMAHAWK, c.1860. Neither Indians nor Europeans used pipe tomahawks before the fur trade. Symbolizing both peace and war, these items combined the symbols of both cultures. This one, collected by a soldier in the Dakota War of 1862, has a blade (7-3/4″ long) with copper inlay on one side and the initials "P.O." on the other. A hickory stem (26-1/2″ long) bears spiral file-burned designs. See color page 63.

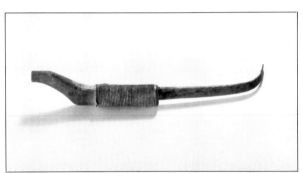

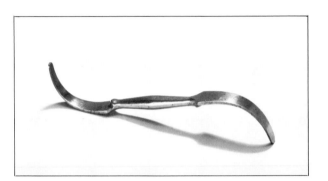

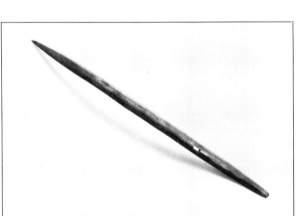

225. CROOKED KNIFE, early 1900s. Crooked knives, made by Sheffield cutlers as early as 1750, were used for making canoes and other woodwork. They worked so well that they are still manufactured. This example (10-1/8″ by 1″), collected by ethnologist Frances Densmore at Grand Portage in 1930, was made from a file. The blade is inserted into a hand-carved wooden handle and held by tightly wrapped string. Densmore identified the handle's shape as a ''Hudson Bay'' type.

226. MATTING NEEDLE, mid-1800s? Traders realized that steel implements could replace the long bone needles traditionally used for weaving bulrush mats. This needle (11-1/4″ long), used to thread a horizontal reed weft through the vertical warp reeds, was donated in 1885 by Henry M. Rice, who traded in the upper Mississippi River area during the late 1840s.

227. QUILL FLATTENER, late 1800s? Searching for new products to sell to Indians, Europeans manufactured what they hoped would be laborsaving tools for traditional Indian crafts. For centuries women had been flattening porcupine quills with fingernails and teeth, or with flat antlers or bones. By the mid-1800s traders, particularly in the northern plains, stocked tooled steel implements like this one (9-1/4″ long).

228. PEWTER PIPE BOWL, late 1700s? Despite its Indian style, this pipe (4-1/2″ long by 2-5/8″ high) was probably commercially cast by Europeans to be mounted on a wooden stem like stone versions. Recovered from the Basswood River by the Quetico-Superior Underwater Research Project, the pipe, in two pieces, still contained tobacco. Fragments of similar metal pipes have been found in Great Lakes and East Coast sites.

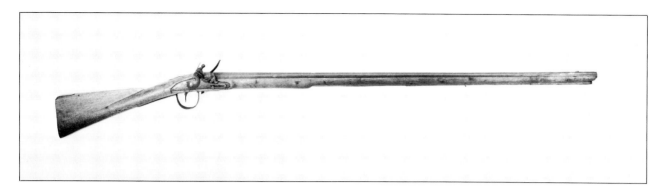

IMPROVING THE MERCHANDISE

Indian consumers demanded the highest quality of merchandise. To satisfy them, merchants and manufacturers searched for better goods and better ways to make them. European technology benefited from developing new solutions to the Indians' problems.

One solution was this gun. Indian hunting methods required lightweight, dependable guns that would stand up to extreme cold. They had to be simple to load and inexpensive. After a century of improvement, British manufacturers arrived at the perfect combination of features. They called it the Northwest gun.

The short barrel of the Northwest gun made it easy to carry in canoes and through the woods. With a wide trigger guard, the gun could be fired while wearing mittens. It had a smooth bore and a distinctive serpent side plate. Its flintlock mechanism was so dependable and easy to repair that Indians preferred it to the percussion rifle well into the 1860s.

Let the guns you send next be not altogether so big in the bore, for the Indians complain of the wideness thereof. Let the bore be of that size as to take a low East India shot and let the grasp of the stock be somewhat smaller than the last, for the Indians complain of the clumsiness of them. You have sent no short guns this year, which are the most in request with the upland Indians which they continually call for and has teased me so about them that it almost distracted me this summer.

—John Fullartine, Fort Albany, 1703

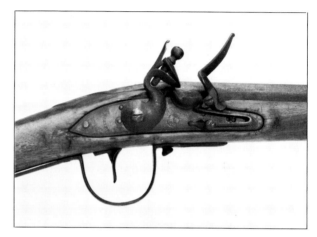

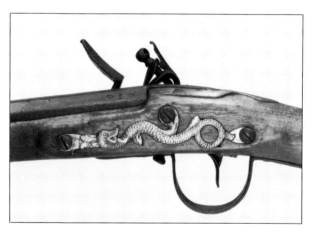

229. NORTHWEST TRADE GUN, c.1800. The marks on this flintlock musket (57-7/8" long) show it was made by gunsmith Robert Wheeler of Birmingham, England. The lock plate bears the "fox in circle" mark. It probably came from the Finger Lakes region of New York. See details.

230. NORTHWEST TRADE GUN, c.1800. Detail.

231. NORTHWEST TRADE GUN, c.1800. Detail.

WHERE DO TWO WORLDS MEET?

232. MIRROR, undated. Archaeologist Jacob V. Brower found this glass mirror set in a hand-made wooden frame near Mandan, N.Dak. Its reflective surface is reportedly mica. The piece (4-1/2" long by 2-1/2" wide by 1/2" deep) may have been recovered during Brower's excavations of trash heaps and abandoned campsites associated with the Mandan Indians near the Heart River, N.Dak. See color page 62.

Where goods changed hands, worlds met as well. This meeting touched each person in a different way. In the fabric of individual lives, cultures blended indiscernibly. In this creative blend, another world was born.

American Indians traded for mirrors like this one in order to see themselves. But the mirror also reflected the images of the Europeans who made it. All artifacts are mirrors in their way. More impartial than words or canvas, they reflect the people who made them, used them, and married two worlds to trade them.

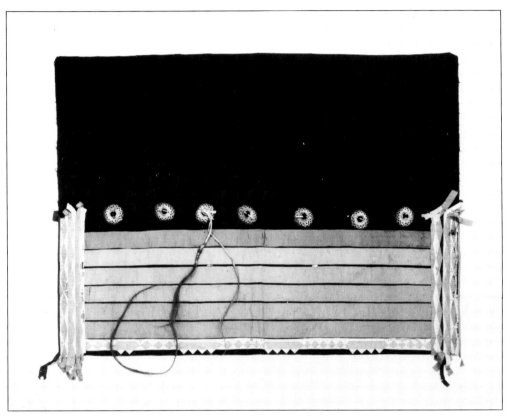

233. BLANKET WITH RIBBON APPLIQUE, pre-1863. This black wool blanket with silk ribbon appliqué was identified by the donor as a child's. It may have been used as a cradleboard cover. One of the seven nickel silver brooches has two strands of hair (a woman's and a child's) attached. Dakota War soldier Charles J. Stees acquired the blanket (35-5/8″ by 25-5/8″) in 1862. It is probably Dakota. See color page 60.

For some people, two worlds met in their families. An Indian mother may have made this blanket to cover her baby's cradleboard. Now the fragile silk ribbons she sewed to the edge are faded and crumbling, but her careful workmanship is still vivid. This intimate gift from an Indian mother to her child is made entirely of European materials. Imperceptibly, the metaphors of two worlds have melted together to bear messages between the generations.

234. YARN BAG, early 1900s. Ethnologist Frances Densmore collected this finger-woven bag (5-1/2" long by 6" wide) in Minnesota before 1930 as an example of traditional Ojibway weaving methods. Such bags were used as containers for personal belongings. See color page 61.

For some people, two worlds met in things they used every day. To make a bag like this, an Indian woman unraveled a white woolen blanket bought from a trader. She colored the yarn with vegetable dyes and rewove the strands by hand in a new pattern and shape. During the fur trade many parts of European life were unraveled by the Great Lakes Indians and rewoven into new patterns. New ideas about time, work, property, land, value, class, and authority all changed and were changed by Indian life.

235. HIDE COAT, mid-1800s. Skin coats modeled on the European cloth coats sold by traders were made by the Ojibway, Cree, and particularly the Red River métis in the early 1800s. Artist Frank B. Mayer, attending an 1851 treaty signing, drew a coat similar to this one, labeling it "winter dress of Red river half-breeds." This one (43-3/4" long at center back by 17-7/8" wide at shoulders) was donated by the granddaughters of Alexander Ramsey, who was at the same treaty signing. It has woven quillwork epaulets and medallions, quillwork embroidery in floral patterns, and both quill-wrapped and beaded fringes. See front and back covers.

Some people were tied to both worlds. The owner of this flamboyant coat may have been a *métis* (mixed-blood) from the Red River Valley. Like the métis themselves, the coat is a mixture: European in style but made of native American materials—cured hide and woven porcupine quills. The coat was given to the Minnesota Historical Society by the granddaughters of Minnesota's first governor. He may have bought it as a souvenir of a trip he made to negotiate an Indian treaty that surrendered part of Minnesota to white settlers.

236. MINNESOTA STATE SEAL, 1849. Originally drawn by Seth Eastman, better known for his illustrations of Indian life, the Minnesota state seal expresses the attitude of most 19th-century Americans toward the meeting of worlds.

By the 1800s Americans of European heritage had made up their minds about their Indian neighbors. Now it seemed to them that the Indians were part of the natural world to be subdued and conquered. They wanted Indian trade and Indian lands, but they could not have both. In the end they chose the land. The economic power of fur traders paved the way for settlement. Thus the fur trade wrote its own death warrant. Soon old traders were running corner groceries, or seeking public office, or moving onto reservations with their friends and families. With the fur trade vanished many paths of communication. The two worlds parted, and their inhabitants, turning away, took separate roads into the future.

APPENDIXES

THE GREAT CARRYING PLACE

Grand Portage

Alan R. Woolworth

A series of five interconnected Great Lakes along the southern rim of the ancient, worn rock of the Precambrian Shield drains into the Atlantic Ocean through the St. Lawrence River. At the far western end of these lakes is the Grand Portage or Great Carrying Place. This nine-mile trail is strategically situated between Lake Superior and another, smaller chain of waterways leading to the northern Great Plains, the Rocky Mountains, and the Athabasca country. During nearly two centuries of fur trade in northern North America, this was second only to Hudson Bay as a natural route into the heart of the continent. (Holmquist and Brookins 1972 : 152)

Indeed, regional geology and geography dominated the water-oriented fur trade from the 17th through the 19th centuries. The 1,200-mile east-west water route of the Great Lakes invited Europeans into the interior of the continent, while no fewer than three geographical features ensured the Grand Portage locality of its place in fur trade history: A deep, sheltered bay with a level shore provided a perfect spot for building trade facilities; a relatively short and easy portage bypassed the rapids and waterfalls of the lower Pigeon River; and the upper river itself was an excellent natural waterway to the west. These advantages led the British North West Company to establish headquarters at the eastern end of the portage on the shore of Lake Superior. From there the company controlled a fur trade empire

Alan R. Woolworth, a Minnesota Historical Society research fellow, was museum curator from 1960 to 1968, chief of the museum and historic sites departments in 1968 and 1969, and the Society's chief archaeologist from 1970 to 1980. Long a student of the fur trade, he has directed archaeological excavations at and been deeply involved in research on the Grand Portage National Monument since 1960.

that spanned the continent by the late 1790s. (Buck 1965 : 26; E. Morse 1969 : 4; Holmquist and Brookins 1972 : 152)

For centuries before the first white man saw the Grand Portage in about 1660, Indian peoples inhabited the region. Because of its infertile soil and short growing season with harsh winters, food resources were limited and populations were small and scattered. Heavy stands of deciduous trees and some mixed conifers rose from the uneven glaciated surface, which was marked by rock outcrops, swamps, inland lakes, and streams. The inhabitants depended on a variety of food supplies—maple sugar in spring, fruits in summer, wild rice in fall, and fish and animals taken throughout the year. (Cleland 1966 : 9–11)

In the late 17th century Cree and Assiniboine Indians lived in the area, but they soon withdrew to the north and west. About 1680 a group of Ojibway Indians left their people at the outlet of Lake Superior and gradually moved—probably accompanied by French traders—around the north shore to Thunder Bay, the mouth of the Pigeon River, and Grand Portage Bay. Their numbers increased at Thunder Bay because of plentiful food resources, and by 1731 some Ojibway probably were living at Grand Portage Bay. (Warren 1885 : 83) Explorer Jonathan Carver noted 35 years later: "The country at the Grand Portage is owned by a chief of the Chipeways (Ojibway) who has a large house and a few warriors here." Carver found food scarce that fall and had to obtain fish and wild rice from the Indians. (J. Parker 1976 : 15)

The intrepid French traders-explorers, Pierre Esprit Radisson and Médard Chouart, sieur de Groseilliers, probably used the Grand Portage as early as 1660 (Sulte 1896 : 167). In 1722, Jean-Daniel-Marie Viennay-Pachot, a French official, wrote of a beautiful trail leading to the Pigeon River (Margry 1886:9). Documented French use of the Grand Portage, however, began in August 1731 when Pierre Gaultier de Varennes, sieur de la Vérendrye, landed at the bay. He attempted to ascend the trail with mutinous voyageurs who thought it too difficult a route and who did not wish to venture farther into an uncharted wilderness. La Vérendrye improved the trail and probably built a small storage facility at the eastern end of the portage in the summer of 1732. During the next two decades, La Vérendrye or his sons appear to have expanded their encampment into a small post with a dwelling, a blacksmith shop, and a warehouse (Burpee 1931:364).

La Vérendrye had traders at the portage in 1739 and again in 1742. In 1750 a trader named St. Pierre traveled to the bay for supplies and powder. Possibly a powder magazine also had been built there. At about this time the elder La Vérendrye died, and the family fortunes declined. Grand Portage Bay continued to serve as a French *entrepot* into the interior for another decade. Traders were sent there in 1751 for two years; another agreed to go there from 1753 until 1756. The spring of 1761 found Joseph Varin La Pistolette trading at the bay. (Burpee 1968:383, 448; Legardeur 1886:clix–clxix; Engagements 1687–1777)

Colonial New France fell to British musketry before walled Quebec in 1760. For a few years thereafter the northwestern fur trade was in a state of chaos. The French abandoned most of their posts in the west, while Pontiac, the Ottawa leader, fired his warriors to resist the British successors until 1765. But Great Britain's merchants and leaders had a mercantile philosophy, sound financial support, and organizational capabilities. The country's expanding industrial base was ready to produce goods for a world market, including the North American Indians. So, during this time, British traders from New England ventured into Canada, where they learned French trading customs based on Woodland Indian technology, subsistence patterns, and traditions. (Innis 1973:166–171; Jackson 1930:231–253)

About 1768, a trader named John Erskine erected a stockaded post at the eastern end of the Grand Portage. Other British traders soon built their own permanent quarters and storage facilities nearby. They employed French voyageurs to paddle large birch-bark canoes of trade goods and supplies from eastern Canada to Lake Superior and the start of the Grand Portage. There innovative merchants such as Laurent Ermatinger hired the idle Montreal laborers to transport 90-pound packs of goods over the nine-mile trail. In such ways the British structured and refined the operations of an expanding northwestern fur trade. (Nute 1940:134; Thompson 1969:24)

The volume of trade had increased remarkably at the portage by 1775, but Alexander Henry the elder found the independent traders "in a state of extreme reciprocal hostility, each pursuing his interests in such a manner as might most injure his neighbour." This unrestrained competition led to furnishing large quantities of liquor to local Indians, and to drunken brawls and murders. As a result, each trader found it prudent to erect a log stockade around his buildings as a means of protection. (N. Woolworth 1975:200)

When trade goods and food became scarce during the American Revolution, the British traders moved their main supply base from Michilimackinac to the Grand Portage. By 1778 furs worth almost 40,000 pounds sterling (equal to about one million dollars today) flowed through Grand Portage warehouses to Montreal and then eastward to European markets. (Rich 1966:72; N. Woolworth 1975:201)

As the small outpost grew, something had to be done to reduce the violent competition between rival traders and to keep the loyalty of the local Ojibway Indians clustered about the bay. During 1778 the Crown responded to traders' urgings by sending a small unit of the King's Eighth Regiment under Lieutenant Thomas Bennett from Michilimackinac to Grand Portage. There they paraded and demonstrated the authority of the British government. Still another change was afoot. Several independent traders pooled their goods and returns to reduce the fierce and expensive competition. This agreement, the genesis of the North West Company, was regularly renewed until 1783, when the company formally organized. Benjamin and Joseph Frobisher and Simon McTavish assumed leading positions in the new firm. (Innis, 1973:196–198; N. Woolworth 1975)

From 1784 to 1787, Benjamin Frobisher directed the expenditure of large sums building a functional fur trade depot at the eastern end of the Grand Portage. He merged several small trading structures into one large complex enclosed by high palisades. Simultaneously, the North West Company enlarged its storage facilities at the western end of the portage into what became known as Fort Charlotte. Horses and oxen were imported to haul goods in wagons over the rough trail, but the experiment met with little success. With the death of the dynamic, farsighted Benjamin Frobisher in April, 1787, the hard-driving McTavish became head of the North West Company. By

1788 the company had established an advance depot serving the Athabasca Department at Rainy Lake and had begun using small sailing ships instead of Montreal canoes to move trade goods and supplies over the Great Lakes. Business boomed. (N. Woolworth 1975; Innis 1973:200, 219–222, 231, 250)

By 1793 the North West Company depot at the eastern end of the Grand Portage had developed into a large, well-equipped establishment serving a still-expanding northwestern fur trade. According to a young clerk named John Macdonell, the company headquarters was located on a shallow bay about three miles wide that was formed by two prominent ridges called Hat Point and Raspberry Point. Opposite a small island in the center of the bay, the depot stood on a low piece of land rising gently from the shore. Its log palisades were only 15 or 20 paces inland. Directly behind the depot rose a lofty, round sugarloaf hill. (Gates 1965:92–94)

The palisades enclosed 16 structures of cedar or fir whipsawed planks with cedar or pine shingled roofs. Door and window frames, as well as most of the doors, were painted a deep reddish color— "Spanish Brown." There were six storehouses for trade goods or furs, an accounting office, and a mess hall. The remaining eight buildings included shops and some dwellings for the company partners and clerks. A wharf extended into the bay at the front of the depot for loading and unloading

the company's small ships. Massive palisade gates were closed at sunset. Because fire was a constant threat, Montreal laborers directed by a clerk and a guide manned two watchtowers at night. (Gates 1965:93)

At the height of the British fur trade hundreds of men traversed the Grand Portage each summer. Most were Montreal voyageurs required to transport eight 90-pound packs of trade goods up the trail. Many carried two such packs at once. Returning downhill from Fort Charlotte to the depot by the bay, they carried two packs of furs. Although mud made the portage difficult, many voyageurs completed the round trip of 18 miles in about six hours. There were 16 posés or resting places spaced at intervals of from 600 to 800 yards. (Gates 1965:93, 95–97; Lamb 1970:97)

Grand Portage Bay was a lively place indeed in July of each year. Then up to 350 Montreal voyageurs arrived in their great Montreal canoes or in sailing ships to unload supplies and trade goods into the depot's warehouses. Now they could enjoy a few days of welcome rest on the beach to the east of Grand Portage Creek, where many slept under their canoes. It would not be long before they would be bound up the portage burdened with trade goods and supplies. (Lamb 1970:98)

Winterers, the elite of the fur-trade labor force who lived at the western posts, came down the portage carrying only a few personal belongings;

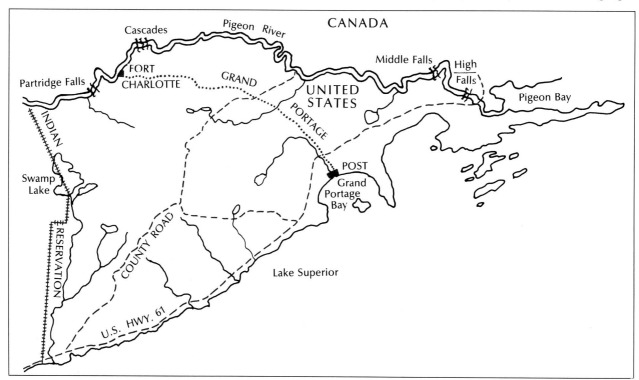

Grand Portage map by Rhoda R. Gilman.

they camped by themselves. This was the time for them to dismiss the months of incredible toil performed at distant trading posts and to revel in the taste of fresh wheat bread, butter, and other treats. It was also a time to dance, carouse, and fight. All too soon they would return up the long portage to their waiting North canoes and the limitless plains and forests.

The rendezvous was not a time of rest for the firm's partners and clerks. Most of the partners spent their time in long meetings with other shareholders in the Great Hall. There they revised company policies to meet changing circumstances, chose members for furloughs, and elevated worthy clerks to the status of partners. (Lamb 1970:79)

In the meantime, the young clerks frantically checked incoming bales of furs, sorted and packed goods and supplies for the winterers, and ran the company's stores. Once these tasks were done, it was their turn to steal a few hours of sightseeing or visiting. Then they, too, would climb the long uphill portage to Fort Charlotte and the wilderness. (Lamb 1957:21-23)

During Simon McTavish's 17-year leadership the North West Company expanded into new regions and increased its stature and profits, and soon a thousand men were participating in the annual Grand Portage rendezvous (Innis 1973:250). In 1797 McTavish's competitors established a rival firm known as the XY Company, and within two years it had built its own depot a few hundred yards east of Grand Portage Creek. The new firm acquired strong leadership and enhanced prestige in 1800, when Alexander MacKenzie, a well-known North West Company partner and explorer, merged his interests with it. Fierce competition between the North West and XY companies ensued. (Thompson 1969:86-93, 104, 109-111)

Although the treaty ending the American Revolution in 1783 had established on paper a boundary between the newly independent colonies and British North America, British traders retained control over much of the Great Lakes region well into the 1790s. As the young American nation began to assert itself, however, it became clear that British days there were numbered. By 1800 the partners of the North West Company decided to move their headquarters to unquestioned British territory. They chose a spot at the mouth of the Kaministikwia River on Thunder Bay, about 45 miles north along the shore of Lake Superior.

Removal from the Grand Portage area was completed by early 1803. A small staff probably remained in the old depot until 1804 or 1805 to oppose the rival XY Company. Late in 1804 McTavish died, making it possible to set aside personal animosity between the two companies. The XY firm held its last rendezvous at the bay in 1805, when it merged with the North West Company. (Thompson 1969:119; Lamb 1970:490; M'Gillivray 1928:70; Lass 1980:17) After that, the Grand Portage was traveled only by local Indians and surveyors, an occasional geologist, and official parties surveying the boundary.

When British traders left, the shores of Grand Portage Bay remained home to a small band of Ojibway Indians. When in need of trade goods they went by canoe to Thunder Bay, where many of their relatives resided. Over the decades they had become largely dependent on the fur trade. Along with many useful articles, traders had furnished liquor with few restraints, and traditional Ojibway social controls had broken down. By this time most white men viewed the Grand Portage Indians as debauched and hostile. Nevertheless, during the War of 1812 some demonstrated their loyalty by serving the British cause, and as late as 1843 they looked upon themselves as British subjects. (Lamb 1957:22; Arthur 1973:33)

In the early 1820s a representative of John Jacob Astor's American Fur Company traded among the Ojibway at Grand Portage Bay. He had a difficult assignment, however. Hudson's Bay Company men from Thunder Bay arrived with supplies on dogsleds and persuaded the Indians to do business with them instead. When the American Fur Company experimented with large-scale salting and shipping of Lake Superior fish in the mid-1830s, Grand Portage became a fishing station with a permanent staff and buildings. But this enterprise was discontinued early in the 1840s. (Buck 1965:34)

A treaty signed by the Lake Superior bands of Ojibway at La Pointe, Wisconsin, in 1854 sold most of the tribe's land bordering the lake. A triangular piece comprising the far northeastern corner of Minnesota between the Pigeon River and Lake Superior was reserved for the Grand Portage Indians. Beginning in the late 1850s, the United States government provided an official farmer, along with agricultural supplies and equipment. But efforts to promote farming failed because of the adverse terrain and harsh climate. Mining and commercial fishing soon began in the region, however, and logging had begun by the close of the 19th century. Many of the Ojibway gradually gave up traditional ways of life as schools taught them to live in a white man's world.

(Buck 1965:35; U.S. Census 1894:353; N. Woolworth 1965:308–310)

By the early 1920s the role that the Grand Portage had played in the North American fur trade had been largely forgotten, except by a few historians. In 1922 Solon J. Buck, superintendent of the Minnesota Historical Society, sent two men to investigate the portage and Fort Charlotte. Buck then wrote a popular account of the area that did much to arouse public interest. It also initiated a continuing concern for this unique fur trade site on the part of the institution. (Buck 1965)

For the past 60 years, staff members and the Society itself have published a steady stream of popular and technical writings about the place. Grace Lee Nute, for example, wrote *The Voyageur* (1931), *The Voyageur's Highway* (1941), and *Rainy River Country* (1950), all kept in print by popular demand. In 1931 the Society helped to reconstruct the wharf in front of the North West Company's depot and commemorated the 200th anniversary of La Vérendrye's landing. In 1936 key staff members worked with the Indian Service Civilian Conservation Corps by supervising various projects in the area. From a small beginning, one undertaking developed into the archaeological excavation of portions of the depot and reconstruction of the palisades and the Great Hall. (*Minnesota History* 1931; A. Woolworth 1980) During World War II the site was neglected, but in 1958 it was donated by the Grand Portage Band of Chippewa (Ojibway) Indians, and Congress established Grand Portage National Monument. The monument includes the partially reconstructed North West Company depot, the nine-mile portage, and the site of Fort Charlotte at the western end of the trail. (Holmquist and Brookins 1972:152)

In the absence of adequate documentation, maps, or contemporary illustrations, archaeological research has been vital to the development and interpretation of this unique locality. So far it has delimited the North West Company depot and its environs, providing basic data on the location, dimensions, function, and construction of several key structures.

Ralph D. Brown was sent by the Society to supervise initial archaeological work by the Civilian Conservation Corps at the depot site in 1936 and 1937. He located the course of more than 1,300 feet of palisades surrounding the two-and-a-third-acre site and determined the location of the Great Hall. Interior trenching in the enclosure revealed the sites of other buildings.

In 1961 the University of Minnesota, under contract with the Minnesota Historical Society, conducted a field school at the monument. Late that year, Alan R. Woolworth, the Society's museum curator, excavated near the monument's eastern border. During the summer of 1962 he made exploratory excavations on a low hill to evaluate it as a site for an interpretive center. The discovery of historic Ojibway Indian burials prevented con-

During 1970 and 1971 the Great Hall site and its surroundings at Grand Portage were thoroughly excavated for the first time. This 1970 northeast view shows the area in front of the hall after it had been stripped of overburden to reveal the piazza's supporting posts. Grand Portage photos by Alan R. Woolworth.

The Great Hall at Grand Portage was reconstructed in 1971 and is now used for on-site interpretation of the fur trade.

struction. At about that time Nancy L. Woolworth began to assist with the fieldwork.

In the 1963 field season the Woolworths directed exploratory excavations around the exterior and interior depot perimeter to guide a more accurate reconstruction of the palisades. A log warehouse site was located northwest of the depot and was fully excavated in 1964. The building was later reconstructed and used for interpretation. The exact position of the main gate in the palisades was found along with other architectural data. After the gatehouse was rebuilt, fieldwork at the monument halted for some years.

Lightning struck the reconstructed Great Hall in July 1969 and it burned. The following autumn, the Woolworths conducted archaeological tests in advance of sewer and water installations. During 1970 and 1971 the Great Hall site and its surroundings were thoroughly excavated for the first time. Little structural data were found aside from the posts that had supported a large veranda in front of the building. The site of a kitchen structure behind the Great Hall produced thousands of domestic artifacts that have greatly enhanced knowledge of late 18th century lifestyles at this location. Both buildings were reconstructed and are used for on-site interpretation.

During 1973 minor excavations within the depot guided placement of sewer and water lines. In 1975 the Society conducted an inventory and evaluation of cultural resources in and around the monument. Fieldwork located what may have

been the site of "Boucher's Fort" about 100 yards east of Grand Portage Creek. Jean Marie Boucher, who was associated with the North West Company, had run a store for company employees from around 1797 to 1802. Evidences of other fur trade structures and an Indian Agency building were found nearby. The Woolworths have continued in recent years to gather and evaluate a variety of historical evidence concerning the Grand Portage area.

The Society conducted underwater archaeological investigations in the Pigeon River off the site of Fort Charlotte at the western end of the Grand Portage in 1963 and 1971 through 1976. These searches also produced a rich harvest of artifacts related to the fur trade era. The portage itself has been upgraded and maintained since 1960, but no archaeological search has been made along the trail. (A. Woolworth 1980, 1981; Wheeler et al. 1975)

The thousands of objects recovered at both ends of the portage have furnished direct empirical evidence of the appearance, functions, and lifestyles of the area's inhabitants. The artifacts already found (many are illustrated in this publication) provide information lacking in historical records, and they are extremely useful in interpreting the history of the Grand Portage. In future years perhaps some of the posés along the trail can be found and investigated by archaeologists. Such investigations would furnish a unique on-site interpretive resource, further enriching our knowledge of the Great Carrying Place.■

THE LA VERENDRYES

Reflections on the 250th Anniversary of the French Posts of La Mer de l'Ouest

Douglas A. Birk

Fifty years ago scholars gathered on Lake Superior's North Shore to commemorate the bicentennial of expanded French presence in the Northwest. The group focused its attention on the well-documented exploits of explorer Pierre Gaultier de Varennes, sieur de la Vérendrye, and his sons, who opened the Grand Portage and lands west to direct European trade in the 1730s (Burpee 1968). Today, as we mark the 250th anniversary of the La Vérendryes' initiative and the golden anniversary of the 1931 meeting, it seems appropriate to determine whether and how our knowledge of the French regime has changed in the past half-century. Are we armed now with new information and explanatory models, or could we celebrate by simply rereading the papers of the 1931 conferees (Kellogg 1931; Burpee 1931)?

The La Vérendryes were among a succession of French-Canadians drawn to the upper Great Lakes region between 1660 and 1760 in search of furs, unchristened souls, and a passage to the "Western Sea." During most of this period Dakota or Sioux Indians occupied the Mississippi headwaters and thwarted French attempts to control or move through their lands. By 1731 it was apparent that the best way both to bypass the Dakota and to capture the interior trade from the Hudson's Bay Company was to move among the Ojibway, Cree, and Assiniboine in the north. Because the La Vérendryes successfully exploited

Douglas A. Birk, a former Minnesota Historical Society archaeologist, has done extensive field and literary research on fur trade, lumbering, and prehistoric aspects of western Lake Superior history. Birk conducted underwater investigations off the shore of Fort Charlotte between 1972 and 1976, and he has more recently completed works on the archaeology of Fort St. Charles and the postrevolutionary British fur trade in the old Fond du Lac district of northern Minnesota and Wisconsin.

this opportunity, their names are firmly identified with early 18th century French activities in the international boundary region. Historians who have pondered their western achievements credit them with "firsts" in bravado, geographic and ethnographic discovery, colonial and missionary advances, and the extension of European agriculture. (Holmquist and Brookins 1972:143–146)

A definitive study of the French regime in the Minnesota area explaining man-land-animal interrelationships from a systemic or ecological viewpoint has yet to be written. Nevertheless, since 1931 economists, historians, and anthropologists have broadened our general understanding of this era. We now more fully realize how few Frenchmen were involved in the French-period trade and how scattered and tenuous their position was in the Indian lands of the Northwest. Researchers today—many of them American Indian—view French presence as a facet of Indian rather than European history. They emphasize that the white man did not "invent" commerce in North America but that he tapped, rearranged, and expanded existing trade networks. Likewise, greater attention has been given to the mutuality of French and Indian cultural exchange and the intensified production of raw and finished materials sought by both groups in the 17th and early 18th centuries. Comparative studies have also shown that European trading establishments shifted from intertribal rendezvous centers to more dispersed tribal and band-level posts as colonial strategies changed and competition for furs increased. (Kellogg 1925; Innis 1973; Eccles 1969; Kavanagh 1967)

In the past half-century many lesser historical details have been uncovered in previously unknown records and through new analysis of those already in hand. Around 1950, for example, state historians first became aware that 1750s journals and correspondence of the French soldier and trader Joseph de la Margue, sieur Marin, were among the collections of a San Marino, California, archive (Nute 1951). From these sources they learned details of Marin's trading and peacemaking forays among Minnesota-area Dakota Indians. They also found that Louis-Joseph, Chevalier de la Vérendrye, who led an expedition across the northern plains in 1742 and 1743, may have wintered at Crow Wing a decade later (Birk 1981).

More recently the Minnesota Historical Society uncovered a significant number of Montreal merchants' business records in Canadian repositories. These exciting documents offer enough information about material culture, economics, and logistics to fuel French-period studies for years. One item copied by archivists attached to the records project is the plan of a French fort said to have been built on Lake Pepin in 1727. Although it is not yet known whether this plan depicts an actual or proposed facility, it is a unique item among the pieces of evidence documenting French presence in the Minnesota area. (White 1977 : 16)

The French left behind another kind of record in the form of archaeological deposits that are only now beginning to receive the scholarly attention they deserve. Ironically, however, because of the incomplete and nonspecific nature of existing written records, few French trade and habitation complexes dating from the period before 1760 have been found. Chroniclers either used what is now archaic terminology or they did not record distances and places at all. As the French sometimes exaggerated the extent and importance of their accomplishments, it is possible that some of their forts were built on a smaller scale or in different areas than claimed. Some may never have been built at all!

Today, as in 1931, the only French-period fort site located and identified by name in Minnesota is Fort St. Charles on the west side of the Lake of the Woods. This depot-trade-habitation-mission complex was the second in a chain of posts that the elder La Vérendrye built or commissioned in the second quarter of the 18th century in "La Mer

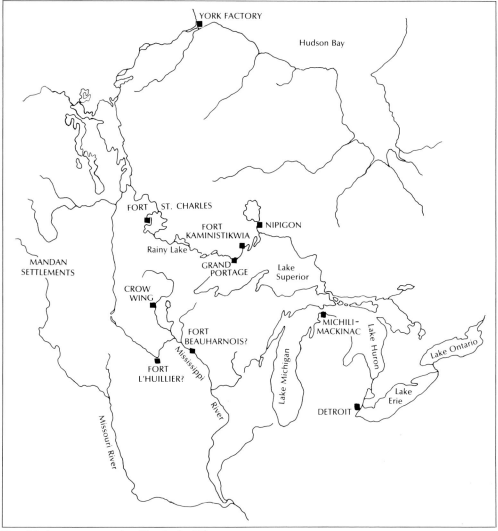

Great Lakes area map by Rhoda R. Gilman.

de l'Ouest," a vast western region centered about Lake Winnipeg. Fort St. Charles served as La Vérendrye's headquarters. Through extended use it became the longest-occupied French post on Minnesota soil. The material record of this site, while not yet fully understood by archaeologists, is one resource that promises to extend our knowledge of French colonial lifeways and interactions far beyond the level of comprehension enjoyed in 1931.

Why were La Vérendrye's Mer de l'Ouest posts built? Why is it that we know the location of Fort St. Charles while the sites of others like forts Beauharnois and L'Huillier in southern Minnesota have escaped discovery? To answer these questions we might first take a closer look at the historical record.

The French regime in the Minnesota area changed along with colonial strategies and the intensity of French involvement during a century of activity. The initial or *French Contact Phase*, which marked the tentative beginnings of western Great Lakes exploration and cross-cultural exchanges between French and local Indian groups, lasted from the mid-1600s to 1700. From around 1700 to 1713 the French largely traded from Hudson Bay and temporarily withdrew from the interior. This made it necessary for Minnesota-area Indians—particularly the so-called middlemen tribes—to transport their furs to more distant rendezvous points like Detroit and York Factory. With the signing of the Utrecht Treaty in 1713 the French lost their position on Hudson Bay and were compelled to resume the interior trade across the Great Lakes. Blocked in the south by the warring Fox and Sauk and the belligerent Dakota, they considered pushing west up the Missouri trench or along the northern height of land that separates Lake Superior from Hudson Bay. During this late or *French Expansion Phase* (1713–1763) the La Vérendryes came into prominence, and the fur trade assumed the characteristics later glamorized by some historians (Birk 1981).

Late-phase French advances into the Minnesota region were hindered by government trade restrictions and by Indians trying to protect their lands from European colonialism and fugitive eastern tribes. Despite these problems, however, the French persisted in their efforts to find the "Western Sea," and by 1722 they were aware of the logistical advantages of pushing to the northwest via Grand Portage. (Innis 1973 : 89)

In 1727, as part of a renewed plan to regularize trade among western tribes, the French built Fort Beauharnois—the one supposedly depicted in the plan found in Canadian business records— somewhere around Lake Pepin. At the same time the elder La Vérendrye was sent to the Nipigon country of northern Ontario where he acquired an Indian map of a water route from Grand Portage Bay to Lake Winnipeg. After spending an isolated winter mulling over the implications of this chart and the rumors of prizes to the west, La Vérendrye was certain that important geographic discoveries lay close at hand. By 1730 his enthusiasm led the governor general of New France to authorize the establishment of the posts of La Mer de l'Ouest. Despite intense lobbying, however, La Vérendrye was denied royal assistance. Instead he was asked to finance his own way to western discoveries by means of a trade monopoly.

Outfitted in Montreal, La Vérendrye arrived at Grand Portage in late August 1731 with a priest, a nephew, three sons, and about 50 soldiers and voyageurs. Apparently when his crew learned of the probable difficulties (including Dakota war parties) on the unimproved overland trail, they rebelled. La Vérendrye had little choice but to send his nephew, Christophe Dufrost de la Jemeraye, on to build a fort at Rainy Lake while he retired with most of his force to Kaministikwia. The following spring matters improved, and the groups reunited at La Jemeraye's Fort St. Pierre before moving on to the Lake of the Woods, where they erected Fort St. Charles. (Prud'homme 1916)

In view of government demands that building elaborate posts not take precedence over the goal of exploration, Fort St. Charles was probably nothing fancy. Contemporary records describe it as a simple palisaded enclosure with two gates, four bastions, and several log cabins or row houses that served as living quarters, storage areas, and a mission (Burpee 1968 : 103; Blegen 1937). The latter structure, as it turned out, proved the key for identifying the remains of the fort in the 20th century.

In the opening decades of the 1700s, the Dakota showed their strength by gaining control of the Rainy Lake–Lake of the Woods area and raiding as far northeast as Kaministikwia. The targets of their raids were the allied tribes of Cree, Monsoni, and Assiniboine who had steady access to French and Hudson's Bay Company firearms (Ray 1974 : 14). When La Vérendrye arrived on the scene in 1731 he upset Dakota control by trading among the northern tribes on contested grounds. In 1736 a Dakota war party retaliated by killing and beheading 21 Frenchmen en route from Fort St. Charles to Michilimackinac. Among the dead were a youthful Jesuit missionary named Jean-Pierre Aulneau and La Vérendrye's eldest son, Jean-Baptiste. La Vérendrye had the bodies of Aulneau and his son "buried in the chapel together with the heads of all the Frenchmen killed" (Burpee 1968 : 227). He also strengthened the fort so that it might be more easily defended.

As a direct result of this incursion, Fort Beauharnois, at Lake Pepin deep in Dakota territory, was immediately abandoned. Coincidentally, the Lake Superior Ojibway, fearing for their middleman trade position, broke relations with the Dakota and realigned with the northerly Cree and Assiniboine. In the following decades the Ojibway gained enough strength to displace the Dakota from northern Minnesota and Wisconsin, possibly with the assistance of French guns (Warren 1885).

Meanwhile, ignoring harassment from the Dakota, the government, and his financial backers, La Vérendrye extended his chain of forts as far west as the Saskatchewan country. At the same time he visited the Mandan settlements on the Missouri River and sent two sons on an expedition across the northern plains (Smith 1980). By 1744, however, the government, convinced that La Vérendrye's deeds were mostly self-serving, forced him to withdraw as commander of the posts of La Mer de l'Ouest. Although his position was later restored, La Vérendrye died in 1749 before he could return to Fort St. Charles. The fort was thereafter administered by other officials until eastern wars forced its closing. By 1760 the French were defeated in battle, and the French regime in the Minnesota area ended abruptly with the signing of the Treaty of Paris in 1763.

Modern interest in Fort St. Charles grew out of the Jesuits' desire in the late 1880s to find and mark the grave of the martyred Father Aulneau. After several visits to the Lake of the Woods, a group of Jesuit instructors from St. Boniface College, Manitoba, finally located the fort site in 1908 (Prud'homme 1916). Steadfast interest, the availability of written records, access to local Indian traditions about the fort, and the undeveloped location of the site area resulted in their success. French fort sites elsewhere in the state are generally not so well documented, or they may lie in areas heavily altered by more recent forms of land use or in areas without Indian inhabitants. Nor have many archaeological surveys been conducted with the drive and determination of the Jesuits.

The skeletal remains of the 21 Frenchmen killed in 1736, unearthed during the Jesuit excavation, furnished irrefutable evidence of the site's identity. All but the bodies of Jean-Baptiste La Vérendrye and Father Aulneau were heaped in two common graves. From the position of these burials the Jesuits were able to determine the general size of the chapel and its relation to other structures in the fort compound.

While it did establish the location of the site, the antiquarian excavation of 1908 must be listed as one of many destructive forces befalling archaeological deposits at Fort St. Charles. A series of dams built at the Lake of the Woods outlet in the 1880s transformed much of the immediate shoreline into a waterlogged marsh. Post-1950 efforts by the Knights of Columbus to make the site into a religious shrine and park did even greater damage. While historians and other scholars remained conspicuously silent, well-meaning Knights cleared and leveled many of the fragile, data-laden deposits with shovels, dynamite, and a bulldozer (Tegeder 1979 : 88, 95, 98, 111, 133, 149). It is almost certain that a full two-thirds of the archaeological record of Fort St. Charles has been destroyed. Only the Jesuit accounts remain to hint at what has been lost. Numerous other French-regime sites in the Great Lakes area have fared no better. For example, in one weekend unorganized diggers armed with pointed rods, spades, shovels, and pickaxes laid to waste an important French fort site near Trempealeau, Wisconsin, shortly after its discovery in 1887.

And so, have we learned anything new in the past 50 years? Since 1931, and especially since 1960, historic archaeology has made tremendous strides in dealing with the material record. Archaeologists have come to understand and treat sites as primary and nonrenewable sources that can be read independently of or in conjunction with written records (e.g., Deetz 1977). Their excavation of early historic sites can now significantly change how we view European colonialism, historic man-land relationships, and even ourselves.

One of the most important of our changing perceptions of the French regime is recognition that some of the last great untapped repositories of early cultural history and process lie at our feet, rather than in dusty and inaccessible archives halfway around the world. The challenge is to insure that those material repositories are handled and studied with the utmost care. We should not complain about what has been lost at Fort St. Charles, but should instead rejoice in what remains. Even one-third of what the La Vérendryes left there might double our knowledge of what they did. ■

PARISIAN WOMEN'S DOGS

A Bibliographical Essay on Cross-Cultural Communication and Trade

Bruce M. White

It is easy when writing about the fur trade to make a fetish of furs, canoes, guns, and other aspects of fur trade material culture, to think of the fur trade as some exotic occurrence the like of which will not be seen again. Such attitudes, however, are evidence of a peculiar blindness. Why should we study the fur trade at all if only to escape the boredom of computerized and mechanized lives? What deeper understanding can we obtain by studying the human reality of the fur trade?

"But They Wear No Breeches!"

In the 19th century travel came into its own as a literary act. No longer simply a means by which a person could see the world for his own pleasure or profit, it became the first step in the publishing process. Now that the technologies of transportation and printing were being perfected, a person could travel safely to distant places and then publish a book, describing the wonders, dangers, and savages on the other side of the globe. So great was the association between books and travel that the word *discovery* signified as much the traveler's account as what he had seen. Indeed, in regard to fur trader William Morrison's claim that he had visited the source of the Mississippi River before Henry R. Schoolcraft, historian William Watts Folwell remarked: "The claim may well be just, but the failure to make any report or record, and a silence of forty years or more, debars Morrison from credit as an exploring discoverer" (Folwell 1922 : 116).

Bruce M. White, a Minnesota Historical Society editor, compiled The Fur Trade in Minnesota: A Preliminary Guide to Manuscript Sources *(1978) and with Douglas A. Birk coauthored "Who Wrote the 'Diary of Thomas Connor'? A Fur Trade Mystery" (1979). He wrote both this essay and "'Give Us a Little Milk': The Social and Cultural Meanings of Gift Giving in the Lake Superior Fur Trade," (1981) during a year's sabbatical leave under a grant from the Society's Charles E. Flandrau Research Fund. White continues to write socioeconomic case studies of fur trade families in the Lake Superior area begun during this leave.*

Besides establishing the reputations of authors, print often gave credibility to wild inventions, allowing writers to magnify the incidents of short visits into elaborate theories about civilizations. But like present-day tourists concluding too much from central heating, toilet paper, and bathtubs, 19th-century sightseers too often judged people not on their moral values, but on the way they managed the technology of ordinary life. This common *technocentrism*, more than anything else, explains the reaction of Europeans to American Indians, whose manners, technology, and material culture were quite different from their own.

These people did not wear European-style clothing, use tables and chairs, live in brick and stone and wood-frame houses, or use printing presses. So Europeans concluded that the Indians were very poor, that they had no manners or history or literature, and that they lived unsettled lives. In short, they were uncivilized. (E.g., Morse 1857 : 339) Such travelers were continuing to act out the prejudices attributed by French philosopher Michel de Montaigne to Europeans over 200 years before. "We call barbarous," he said, "that which is different from our own way of doing things"* (Montaigne 1958 : 234). Writing of certain admirable qualities of South American Indian society, Montaigne had unknowingly set the pattern for what would later pass as accurate reporting on American Indians: "All this is not bad, but they wear no breeches!"* (Montaigne 1958 : 245). He later stated his own opinions about clothing: "If we were born with the need for petticoats and breeches, nature would no doubt have armed with a thicker skin those parts that she exposes to the rigours of the season, just as she has done the finger-tips and the soles of the feet" (Montaigne 1978 : 120).

Philosophers were more likely than most travelers to learn from distant cultures. By comparing

*Author's translation from the French.

120

widely different ways of life and seeing European society with the eyes of foreigners as did Montesquieu (1980) in his imaginary *Persian Letters*, these Europeans could put their own institutions to the test. Unfortunately, philosophers did not shape the general cultural view. And since Europeans controlled the printing presses, the reactions of American Indians to European civilization were seldom published. The few that were, made fascinating reading and gave smug Europeans a chance to know what it was like to be discovered themselves.

Artist George Catlin (1848) recounted his travels through England and France with American Indians in the early 1840s. The trip's ostensible purpose was to give Europeans an opportunity to observe some of the exotic peoples their countrymen had been writing about for so long. But it also provided the Indians with a rare chance to see the source of their own peculiar invaders. Fortunately Catlin, a stranger in Europe himself, spent much of his time recording the reactions of the Indians to Europeans rather than the other way around.

The Indians were surprised, awed, and disgusted. Through visits to coal mines, factories, breweries, ginshop-lined streets, trains, and city slums, they were able to compare technological prodigiousness with the widespread lack of social welfare evident in Europe during the Industrial Revolution. However, as in the case of most 19th-century travelers, the small things impressed the Indians most—the peculiar ways in which Europeans handled the mundane parts of their lives.

A group of Iowa Indians visiting Paris was most puzzled by the phenomenon of Parisian women's dogs. Wherever the Indians went, they saw women walking the streets with dogs of all sizes—on strings, in the women's arms, or running freely around their skirts. One day two Iowa decided to make a record of the dogs just as they made records of executions, drunkards, paupers, and other aspects of European life. After an hour they had recorded statistics strangely reminiscent of those being published in contemporary works on American Indians:

- Women leading one little dog   432
- Women leading two little dogs   71
- Women leading three little dogs   5
- Women with big dogs following (no string)   80
- Women carrying little dogs   20
- Women with little dogs in carriages   31

(Catlin 1848 : 221)

Why, the Iowa wondered, did these dogs receive so much consideration and attention? Why did the saleswoman from whom they tried to purchase a dog for a traditional feast treat them with such horror? Why were these dogs coddled when the orphanages were full of unwanted children? Parisians had much wonderful technology, but they treated dogs better than children! (Catlin 1848 : 257–260)

The Debits and Credits of Communication

Frederick Jackson Turner began his Ph.D. thesis on the fur trade of Wisconsin with Montesquieu's remark that "the history of commerce is the history of the intercommunication of peoples" (Turner 1977 : 2). The fur trade, more than any other way in which Europeans and American Indians took one another's measure, thrived on communication—not simply through a language of words, but also through a language of objects. (See also Renfrew 1975.)

A most useful text for understanding the nature of commerce in the fur trade is that often misunderstood record of human relationships, the business account book. Within the precisely coded and quantified record of debits and credits in journals and ledgers recording transactions between traders and Indians (see below)—of Indian furs, snowshoes, meat, wild rice, corn, and canoes traded for European blankets, clothing, jewelry, guns, shot, tobacco, and rum—is the essence of the fur trade. Yet the very precision of such account books often disguises the social and

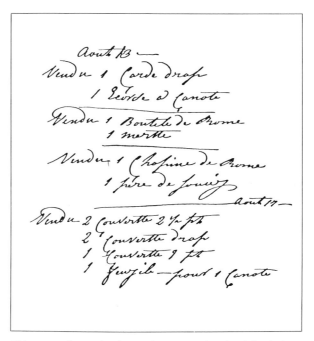

This entry from the journal account book of Sault Ste. Marie trader Jean Baptiste Barthe records transactions with American Indians in 1776. The Indians traded birch bark, moccasins, a canoe, and one marten skin for cloth, rum, blankets, and a gun. Burton Historical Collection of the Detroit Public Library.

cultural nature of an activity involving many threads of human society. In fact, these objects had as much ambiguity and cultural meaning as Parisian women's dogs.*

Merchandise and furs did not trade themselves. There was nothing automatic about the process. The trader arriving at an Indian community with a load of trade goods could not expect to barter for furs immediately. In order to do business, the trader often needed to know the Indian language. But he probably needed even more to know the Indian meanings of things: the customs, modes of behavior, and cultural values of his intended customers. Only then could he establish equivalents between Indian and European cultural worlds. Only then could he translate from a society in which dogs might be feasted upon to one in which dogs might be treated like people. How could such different cultural languages be reconciled? What social processes had to come into play in order for trade to take place?

Implicit in these questions is the assumption that economic exchanges were only a small part of the much more complicated fur trade process. Each transaction took place in what Arthur J. Ray has called "the system of institutions, relationships, and processes which permitted two highly dissimilar cultural groups—the Indian and the European, to maintain continuous trade over an extended period of time" (Ray and Freeman 1978 : xv).

Ray, whose sophisticated work in the rich business records of the Hudson's Bay Company sharpens our understanding of these institutions, relationships, and processes, has conceived a model revealing the intricacy of the fur trade process. The abstraction of Ray's model (see right) shows the extent of economic relationships in the Hudson's Bay Company's trade. The reciprocal process of trade was made possible only by the creation of a vast Indian-European economic framework (Ray 1974).

Of course, as Toby Morantz (1980 : 57) has pointed out, there were many fur trades, and we need separate models to describe the trade in other areas, such as the Great Lakes or the Rocky Mountains. In such different circumstances Indian middlemen might be replaced by lower-level white or métis traders living close to Indian villages. Or the company in London might be replaced by a supplier in Montreal.

---

*"Value, therefore does not stalk about with a label describing what it is. It is value, rather that converts every product into a social hieroglyphic. Later on, we try to decipher the hieroglyphic, to get behind the secret of our own social products; for to stamp an object of utility as a value, is just as much a social product as language" (Marx 1967 : 74).

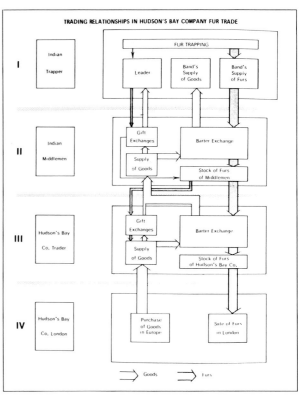

Arthur J. Ray's model (1974 : 46) shows the extent of trading relationships in Hudson's Bay Company trade.

In all these fur trades, however, economic activities were only one thread in an elaborate fabric of interaction involving the trade of tangible and intangible commodities. Not just furs, trade goods, and supplies, but also information, languages, loyalties, and people were part and parcel of the economic process. In two recent pathbreaking studies on families, children, and women in the fur trades of the North West and Hudson's Bay companies, Jennifer S. H. Brown (1980) and Sylvia Van Kirk (1980) have shown that intercultural marriages were not simply a solution to the demands of desire in the wilderness. Marriage and kinship had an economic role as little understood in its importance to the fur trade as to other facets of European and North American economic life.

Advancement through family relationships was not an exclusively Indian-influenced process. A proper marriage could be an important way for a trader to strengthen economic ties with his own merchant class just as it might improve the standing of the trader within Indian society. (J. Brown 1980) Marriage was just as important a part of economic tie-making as were the legal contracts between voyageurs and fur companies or among independent traders creating the extended partnership of the North West Company (Wallace 1934).

The Empire of Happiness

Around 1805, Roderick McKenzie, a chief Montreal partner in the North West Company, prepared to send a printed circular to his fellow partners and traders in the western country. It provided a list of topics on which he wished to gather information about the Indians with whom the company traded.

Gathering information on customers had always been an important part of fur trade record-keeping for the rival Hudson's Bay Company. By reading the letters and diaries of traders, management could keep better track of changing fur trade conditions. But McKenzie's purpose was different. He hoped to benefit mankind by writing a book that compared Indian societies with what was known of other peoples around the world. "By extending the bounds of knowledge and of industry," a draft of the circular began, "we increase the empire of happiness; He who makes us acquainted with what we know not before, is surely a benefactor to his kind; and he who supplies a want which another feels, tho interest may direct his diligence, will always be estimable in the scale of polished society" (R. McKenzie 1805 : 2). McKenzie knew that despite their supposedly overriding mercenary interest, traders were in a unique position to provide information on Indian society.

McKenzie's book was never published, but many drafts of it have been preserved in the Public Archives of Canada. Its four sections on America, Asia, Europe, and Africa include a series of extracts largely based on McKenzie's extensive reading of published travelers' narratives, with a smattering of entries from traders' diaries. The work's numerical and thematic arrangement enables the reader to compare very specifically the customs of American Indians with those of other peoples.

Today many of the extracts say less about the nature of human societies than about the superficiality of 19th-century travelers. Extract 52 from the section on travels through Asia shows why it is perhaps fortunate that McKenzie's entire work has not been published: "The people to the south are a savage race and go almost naked. A woman guilty of adultery is thrown to an elephant who destroys her. A man may sell his wives and children. They burn the dead and deposit the ashes in urns. They go in mourning from three to six months" (R. McKenzie n.d.).

Historians nevertheless owe McKenzie their gratitude—not for what he might have considered his crucial contribution, but because he was so successful in collecting the writings of fur trad-ers. Portions of his collection were finally edited and published in *Les Bourgeois de la Compagnie du Nord-Ouest* in 1889 and 1890 by Louis R. Masson (1960), the son-in-law of McKenzie's son Alexander. In the absence of substantial surviving collections of early North West Company business records, these materials, whether in published or manuscript form, are the source of much of the written history of the firm.*

In addition many anthropologists and ethnohistorians such as Harold Hickerson (1959) have found his collections (and others like those at the Hudson's Bay Company Archives) an excellent source of information about Indian society. Seldom matched by the superficial narratives of travelers, the traders' writings are rich in cross-cultural insights brought about by the need to communicate on many levels. For instance, trader Charles McKenzie (1809) wrote of an incident during his stay among the Cheyenne and Mandan Indians along the Missouri River in 1805. Two important North West Company traders of the Red River department, Charles Chaboillez and Alexander Henry the younger, visited McKenzie in hope of buying horses from the Indians.

The traders' first words reproached McKenzie for his clothing, "the Indian costume of that quarter." In one version McKenzie defended himself for what his superiors found to be a social error: "Let the idea of Savage be taken away and this dress will be considered more *suitable* than any other to my situation and circumstances at the time. With this dress I could pass and repass as often as I pleased through the villages unmolested; whereas a Christian or civilized dress would subject me not only to the notice, but often to the gaze and even to the ridicule of the Natives and the attack of all the Village curs" (C. McKenzie 1809 : 167). (It is clear that dogs, not content to be passive "social hieroglyphics," are themselves students of human cultural language.)

In Masson's version (1960), McKenzie went on to describe the effects of his superiors' inability to understand the Indians' particular language of clothing. When he told the Indians that these unshaven, dirty traders in weather-beaten coats and hats were important, they did not believe it. How could Chaboillez and Henry be "chiefs"? In words that could as well apply to the modern businessmen who made necessary the book

---

*It is unfortunate that Masson garbled and slashed almost every manuscript that he published. A new edition of his work, based on original manuscripts in the Public Archives of Canada and at McGill University, is badly needed. Charles M. Gates (1965) did a more creditable job of editing some of the McKenzie manuscripts.

Dress for Success (Molloy 1976), McKenzie concluded: "Men of dignity must deck themselves better than the common voyageur if they wish to be considered as they should be. As the Indians have no idea of mental abilities, there must be some thing in the outward appearance to attract notice and command respect" (Masson 1960 : 385).

Obviously the fur traders were creatures of their time, sharing many European prejudices both favorable and unfavorable. As Lewis O. Saum's comparative study (1965) has shown, the writings of fur traders must be carefully used. Some traders were like the younger Alexander Henry, who, in the words of his editor Elliott M. Coues, "had no sympathy with [the Indians] whatever. They were simply the necessary nuisances of his business, against whom his antipathies were continually excited and not seldom betrayed in his narrative. He detested an Indian as much as he despised a Franco-Canadian voyageur, or hated a rival of the H.B. or X.Y. Company" (Coues 1897 : xviii). (Coues seems to think that Henry's very prejudice made him likely to be accurate.)

There were other traders, however, who after long years in the western country had a different view—one based on acceptance of the Indians as human beings with different ways of doing things. Perhaps more than any other Northwester, clerk George Nelson understood and appreciated Indian culture. About Indian folktales he remarked: "I was often much amused & highly entertained with their stories which they would frequently tell in the evenings. The exhortations to their children much pleased me—they were truly edifying. There was nothing of course in them relative to the atonement by our Saviour, but their discourses were full of strong argument, beautiful comparisons & allegories, & most pathetic appeals to the understanding as well as to the *feeling*. . . . I don't know that I have heard [a sermon] yet in this country [Lower Canada] to come up to the many I have heard above. But I must not offend the pride of our educated folks here. Their dignity would be shocked by the comparison, tho' in substance they are far behind these children of the Forest" (Nelson n.d. : 50).

Nelson's attitude toward the Indians had much to do with the fact that he spent his years in the fur trade not in acquiring wealth but in gaining self-knowledge. This made him more able than most to learn about other people. Eventually he reached a philosopher's understanding of the relativity of cultures; in a reference to life in eastern Canada he put the word *civilized* in quotation

marks followed by a parenthetical exclamation point (Bardon and Nute 1947 : 145). But Manifest Destiny was the order of the day, and such views of Indians and Europeans were not widespread. Much of Nelson's well-written, richly detailed, and compelling work still awaits publication.*

Schoolcraft's "Discovery"

In 1821 another circular traveled from an eastern city to outposts of white society in the west. More elaborate than McKenzie's, its purpose was the same: to obtain information about the Indians. This one was sent not by an economic capitalist, but by a politician. Lewis Cass, the governor of Michigan Territory, had addressed it to the agents in his jurisdiction.

Although Cass was as interested as any member of his social class in the removal of American Indians from their land, he had an amateur's interest in their way of life. He felt that Indian culture should be recorded before it passed away in front of "the advance of civilization." His questions, though useful, betray many prejudices, and today they have all the surrealism of the study questions in a high school textbook. Under the heading "General Manners and Customs," he asked:

- Do they ever eat human flesh, and if so, upon what occasions and with what ceremonies?
- What is their mode of salutation when they meet?
- What do they say on these occasions?
- Is shaking hands an Indian custom and if not, what analogous custom have they?
- Is any particular respect paid to age or rank?
- Do they ever visit one another for the purpose of conversation?
- Do they have regular parties at which they entertain one another?
- Are they in the practice of telling stories?

(M. Williams 1974 : 291)

This last question was to be the preoccupation of Henry Schoolcraft, one of Cass's most active agents. He would over the following years publish many American Indian folktales, most of them for the first time.** Schoolcraft's researches into the literature of American Indians were for many (including himself) a revelation. "What have all the voyagers and remarkers from the days

---

*In papers presented at the Fourth North American Fur Trade Conference, Sylvia Van Kirk (1981) and Jennifer Brown (1981) brought much deserved attention to George Nelson's writings. It is hoped that they will succeed in bringing about the publication of a complete edition of his work.

**It is not Schoolcraft's fault that these collections of folktales should have inspired Henry Wadsworth Longfellow's cultural hodgepodge, *The Song of Hiawatha* (1855).

of Cabot and Raleigh been all about," Schoolcraft wondered, "not to have discovered this curious trait [telling stories], which lifts up indeed a curtain, as it were, upon the Indian mind, and exhibits it in an entirely new character?" (M. Williams 1974 : 308)

But Schoolcraft's discovery was not an independent one. With the guidance of trader John Johnston and his wife, O-shaw-gus-co-day-way-quah, the daughter of Lake Superior Ojibway chief Waubojeeg, Schoolcraft began to learn about Indian oral literature. Three days before his entry about the discovery of this "fund of fictitious legendary matter," Schoolcraft had written in his diary: "Mrs. Johnston is a woman of excellent judgment and good sense; she is referred to on abstruse points of the Indian ceremonies and usages, so that I have in fact stumbled, as it were, on the only family in North West America who could, in Indian lore, have acted as my 'guide, philosopher, and friend'" (M. Williams 1974 : 308).

Although both Schoolcraft and the Johnstons were unique in their dedication, many Great Lakes historians, travelers, government agents, and anthropologists also had benefited from a mode of cross-cultural communication established by the fur trade. Even as thorough an ethnographer of the Ojibway as Joseph N. Nicollet depended throughout his travels on fur traders (M. Bray 1970; E. Bray and M. Bray 1976).

Many of the "guides, philosophers, and friends" were métis. Jacqueline Peterson (1978) has noted in her study of the Great Lakes métis community that this group, which had its origins in the fur trade, played an important intermediary role that went beyond the fur trade. Anthropologist John S. Wozniak's intricate study (1978) of the Eastern Dakota has shown that fur trade and Indian family connections often made possible the implementation of United States government policy. Ironically, this intermediary role aided the government in dispossessing American Indians.

It is as interpreters and as cultural and political middlemen in such government efforts that the fur traders and their families really fit into the story of the European "settlement" of North America. They were not, as commonly suggested, part of some monolithic attempt to make Indians "dependent" on European manufactures in order to destroy them. From the perspective of the fur traders, "settlement" was simply an afterthought. The removal of American Indians from their land—the worst of the many terrible things done to them—was as much contrary to the interests of the fur trade as it was to the health and cultural well-being of the Indians.

How Did It Work?

Fur trade historians have traditionally sought to place the trade within larger European and North American contexts. Without always clearly defining the fur trade or spending much time on the people and processes involved, they have tried to explain it in relation to broad themes of history.

For historian Harold A. Innis (1973) the fur trade was the exploitation of one staple resource in the economic development of Canada, part of a litany that included fish, lumber, and wheat.* American "settlement" historians like Frederick Jackson Turner saw the fur trade as one step in the political, social, geographical, and military process of turning America from a "howling wilderness" into nicely plowed farmland and neatly paved cities. As Wayne E. Stevens (1928 : 13) put it in his flawed but valuable survey of the Great Lakes fur trade during the early British period: "The era of the fur trader has usually been a transitory stage in the history of any region, beginning with the penetration of the wilderness by the explorer and hunter, and disappearing before the onward march of the settler."

The work of more recent fur trade historians is less ambitious but perhaps more complicated. Although they have not hesitated to deal at least in passing with the broad significance of the fur trade, their main concern has been with its inner workings.

For earlier historians and for many popular writers on the fur trade the question of how the fur trade worked could be answered by quoting secondary sources. To such sources we owe a large number of commonly accepted understandings that have taken on all the qualities of myth: In the spring of the year the brigades of canoes manned by cheerful, singing, hungover French-Canadian canoemen would set out from Montreal impelled by a spontaneous spirit of adventure in search of the furs that would make them all rich. . . . European manufactures were so useful and attractive to the simpleminded Indians that they paid enormous prices to traders and quickly abandoned their own material culture, leading them to lose all their native cultural traditions. . . . Fur traders actuated only by greed quickened this inevitable process by "flooding" the Indian country with rum—the very essence of European civilization that drove

---

*Innis's ideas are simple; only his explanation is complicated. People who use his book as an explanation of the workings of the fur trade forget his purpose, indicated in the subtitle of his book.

primitive man to destruction while making the fur trader wealthy.*

Did any of these things really happen? If they did, do they have the significance they have been given? How was it that European manufactures and Indian products came to be traded, and what impact did this have on all concerned? How, in fact, did the fur trade work?

Much has been done in recent years to pursue these questions. The detailed and useful work of Louise Dechêne in the business records of late 17th and early 18th century Montreal merchants has shown that the contribution of French Canada to the fur trade in the French and British periods is not contained simply in the myth of the voyageur. In addition, Dechêne demonstrated that though it

*Elements of these myths can be found in a wide variety of writings from the newspaper article to the dissertation. Although Grace Lee Nute (1931) fostered the growth of the voyageur myth, her many other studies have shown that she does not have a narrow view of the fur trade. Writers who have fed the myth of drastic cultural change (see Dixon 1980:41) are discussed in an admirable paper given by Donald F. Bibeau (1981) at the Fourth North American Fur Trade Conference. Discussion of the use of liquor in the fur trade (see Jacobs 1972:33–35) is usually marred by temperance rhetoric and the assertion (earlier applied to Blacks and Irish) that Indians could not "handle" liquor. It is time for a dispassionate examination from the perspective of culture, not race.

might very well be said that profits in the fur trade were high (at times matching the 700 percent given by Lahontan in 1690), these were in fact the gross gains of the *entire* fur trade process. From this markup had to be paid a variety of expenses before net profits were divided among shipper, supplier, trader, and others along the way. (Dechêne 1974:163–170)

From the detailed studies of Ray and Morantz, as well as of Charles A. Bishop (1974) and Adrian Tanner (1979), the active and creative role of Indians in the fur trade becomes clear, effectively contradicting the still widespread ideas about Indian victimization and destruction by the fur trade. If this line of inquiry is pursued in primary sources (from the financial records of traders and companies to the oral literature of American Indians), students of the fur trade may reach the goal that George Catlin, Montaigne, the Iowa Indians, Roderick McKenzie, George Nelson, and Henry Schoolcraft sought—a clearer understanding of people and the ways they structure their societies and relate to each other across cultural distances. As historians build their models and construct their pictures of the trade, they may at last find revealed that most enigmatic of texts, the human face.■

Members of two conflicting cultures, each wearing traditional tribal clothing, confront and take the measure of each other in this frontispiece from (George) *Catlin's Notes of Eight Years Travels and Residence in Europe* (1848).

ARTIFACT NOTES

In captions, all place names not further identified are in Minnesota. Where provenance is not given, it is unknown. Dimensions are rounded to the nearest 1/8″. **C.** before a date means plus or minus ten years. **Early 1800s** includes 1800s through 1830s. **Mid-1800s** applies to 1840s through 1860s. **Late 1800s** applies to 1870s through 1890s. Information in captions for which a source is not given below can be found in the MHS museum accession files.

In artifact notes, abbreviations are as follows: **NPS** for National Park Service; **MHS-A** for Minnesota Historical Society Archaeology collection; **MHS-AV** for Minnesota Historical Society Audio-Visual collection; **MHS-L** for Minnesota Historical Society Library; **MHS-M** for Minnesota Historical Society Museum collection; **MHS-MSS** for Minnesota Historical Society Division of Archives and Manuscripts. There are no notes for some artifacts.

1. Engraved cartouche. (Faden 1777:map 3.)
2. Birch-bark box. MHS-M. 6459. (Orchard 1916:51–53; Lyford 1943:120–123; Whiteford 1970:88, 109.)
3. Horn spoons. MHS-M. 66.140, 6516.1. (Whiteford 1970:132.)
4. Bone tools. MHS-M. 4085.A3029 (shuttle), 4981 b, a, c (awls), 67.199.5 (knife). (Brower 1904:xx, xxi; Whiteford 1970:125; Brennan 1975:152, 153; Densmore 1979:169.)
5. Pipe bag. MHS-M. 9999.2. (Whiteford 1970:89; Orchard 1916:10, 11; Lyford 1943:102–104, 120–123.)
6. Pouch. MHS-M. 8034.7.
7. Reed mat. MHS-M. 6988.9. (Densmore 1979:154–156, 184; Lyford 1943:88–95.)
9. Pottery jar. MHS-M. 1171.A590. (Brain 1979:224.)
10. Wooden bowl. MHS-M. 74.101. (Densmore 1979:170; Sweeny sketches, MHS-AV.)
11. Willow basket. MHS-M. 6935.12. (Densmore 1979:162; Lyford 1943:60, 61.)
12. Birch-bark basket. MHS-M. 74.52.8. (Douglas 1941:5–8; Densmore 1928:396; Lyford 1943:46–60.)
13. Clasp knife blade. MHS-A. 388-175-1. (Russell 1977:170–172, 220–223; Birk 1981:personal communication; Stone 1974:262–265.)
14. Harpoon point. MHS-A. 388-51-43. (Stone 1974:277, 278.)
15. Gunflints. MHS-A. 63.65.10. (Wheeler et al. 1975:74, 75; Witthoft 1966:28–35.)
16. Arrowheads. MHS-A. 388-51-11, 388-50-27. (Quimby 1966:65; Birk 1981:personal communication; J. Hanson 1972:4.)
17. Felling ax. MHS-A. 69.195. (Russell 1977:257, 408.)
19. Glass beads. (Woodward 1970:16–18; Orchard 1929:83–85; Quimby 1966:84.)
20. Glass beads. MHS-M. 71.87.1. (Brain 1979:98ff.)
21. "Jesuit rings." MHS-A. 388-50-2, 388-50-3, 388-51-2, 388-51-3, 388-25-5, 388-54-1, 388-51-1. (Brain 1979:192; Stone 1974:123–131; Cleland 1972:202–210; Birk 1981:personal communication.)
23. Flintlock gun. MHS-M. 74.33.2. (Russell 1957:108–113; Hamilton 1980:73.)
24. Gunflints. MHS-A. uncatalogued. (De Lotbiniere 1980:55–69; Vernon and Gonsior 1978:33–47.)
25. Awls. MHS-A. 21CK6 1936 uncatalogued. (Stone 1974:155–159; *Museum of the Fur Trade Quarterly* 1971a:2; J. Hanson 1975:61.)
26. Fire steels. MHS-A. F.P.317, NPS. 21CK6 1963 199-10. (Wheeler et al. 1975:52, 53, 64, 99; Megill 1963:53; Macfie 1962:50, 51; A. Woolworth 1969a:73; 1969b:38; Stone 1974:186–188; Russell 1977:349–355.)
27. Trade ax. MHS-A. 68.49.4(WR 4). (Wheeler et al. 1975:82, 104; Wynn Company 1798–1799.)
28. Knives. MHS-A. uncatalogued, NPS. 21CK6 1964 731, 21CK6 1963 526-3. (H. Peterson 1958:129–131; A. Woolworth 1969a:75, 88; 1969b:100; 1969c:25; Stone 1974:269, 270.)
29. Silver cross. MHS-M. 63.173. (Fredrickson 1980:36; E. Hart 1963:2.)
30. Glass beads. NPS. 21CK6 1963 172-1. (A. Woolworth 1969b:32.)
31. Rings. NPS. 21CK6 1963 561-4, 578-14. (A. Woolworth 1969b:107, 110.)
32. Two metal kettles. MHS-A. FD 155, 156. (Wheeler et al. 1975:58; Macfie 1962:50; Megill 1963:50.)
33. Flintlock gun. MHS-M. 3321.H467. (H. Peterson 1964:322; C. Hanson 1955:26, 36; Russell 1957:126, 139; 1977:63, 68.)
34. Trap. MHS-M. 72.64.71. (*Minnesota History* 1972:146–148; Russell 1977:122, 141; Newhouse 1867:209–213.)
35. Brass kettle. MHS-M. 6385.4. (Kauffman 1968:77–79; *Minnesota History* 1924:506; J. Hanson 1975:59; on the manufacturing process, see Hinckley 1853:201, 202.)
36. Fire steels. MHS-M. 6935.14a. (*Museum of the Fur Trade Quarterly* 1971b:2–4; Russell 1977:351, 352.)
37. Green River knife. (H. Peterson 1958:64–66; Metcalf 1966:4–6; Russell 1977:200; J. Hanson 1975:51, 52; Woodward 1970:65–68.)
38. Ax. MHS-A. 4721. (Brower 1901:49.)
39. Pipe tomahawk. MHS-M. 3625.H503. (H. Peterson 1965:33–39; Woodward 1970:45; J. Hanson 1975:38–40.)
40. Glass beads. MHS-M. 75.47.2. (Good 1977:28–31; Orchard 1929:88, 89; Woodward 1970:22.)
41. Armband. MHS-M. 6221.1. (Woodward 1970:29–31.)
42. Effigy pipe. MHS-M. 69.138.9. (Dunhill 1924:60; West 1934:756.)
43. Effigy pipe. MHS-M. 8070.35. (Beaubien 1955:8, 9.)
44. Club. MHS-M. 301.E97. (Coe 1977:180; Casagrande and Ringheim 1980:68.)
45. Horn spoon. MHS-M. 6015.2. (*Pioneer Press* 1955; Ferguson 1954.)
46. Pipe. MHS-M. 7059.98.
47. Effigy pipes. MHS-M. 3693.A2697, 3696.A2700. (Winchell 1911:483, 484; Cleland 1971:87.)
48. Umbilical cord case. MHS-M. 9859.29. (Densmore 1979:51; Lyford 1943:102–104.)
49. War club. MHS-M. 66.104.5. (J. Hanson 1975:36–38; Childs 1905:850; J. Williams 1876:399.)
50. *A Beaver 26 inches . . .* (Lahontan 1905:frontispiece.)
51. Beavers. (Le Beau 1738:facing p. 320.)
52. *Beavers Building Their Hutts.* (Smart et al. 1760:11.)
53. *The Beaver.* (Du Creux 1951:77.)
55. *Spearing Muskrats in Winter.* (Eastman 1853:facing p. 58.)
56. Metal trap. MHS-M. 72.64.70. (*Minnesota History* 1972:146–148; Russell 1977:102–144; Rolette 1835.)
58. Spear. MHS-M. 8643.2. (J. Hanson 1975:31–35.)
59. Bow and arrows. MHS-M. 8110.1, 67.199.8a–f. (Ferguson

1954; on use of bows and arrows see Copway 1860:35–37, 62, 66; J. Tanner 1956:13, 170.)

60. Muskrat spears. MHS-A. LQP H51a, uncatalogued. (Wheeler et al. 1975:72–74; Russell 1977:321–325.)

61. *A Beaver Pool.* (Lahontan 1905:facing p. 556.)

62. Trap. MHS-M. 4696. (A. Harding 1907:51, 52; Russell 1977:122, 141.)

63. *The Beaver.* (Newhouse 1867:facing p. 42.)

64. Ice chisel blades. MHS-A. 68.49.5(WR36), uncatalogued, 68.49.5(WR35). (Wheeler et al. 1975:70–72, 105; D. Parker 1966:88, 89.)

65. Ax. MHS-A. uncatalogued. (Russell 1977:268.)

66. Snare wire. MHS-A. 63.65.12. (Wheeler et al. 1975:14.)

67. Trade gun. MHS-M. 3320.H466. (Carey 1953:70; Russell 1957:116–118, 137; 1977:68–70, 72–75; C. Hanson 1955:47; Peirce 1962.)

68. Gun equipment. MHS-M. 69.51 (shot pouch and powderhorn); MHS-A. 63.65.1 (musket balls); MHS-A. 64.179.3 (shot); NPS. 21CK6 1963 173-5 (gun worm); NPS. 21CK6 1963 94-8, 564-5 (files); MHS-A. 68.49.2(WR66, 131, 128) (files).

71. Trade axes. MHS-A. 63.12. (Wheeler et al. 1975:69, 70, 82, 83, 103; H. Peterson 1965:18, 19.)

72. *Indians Trading.* MHS-AV.

73. Shells. MHS-M. 8039.43, 6676.14, 6586.11, 5239. (Whiteford 1970:133, 140; Orchard 1929:20–23.)

74. Copper tools. MHS-A. 1376.A796; MHS-M. 9539.1, uncatalogued; MHS-A. 1461.A881. (Kellogg 1925:345–347; Hunt 1940:17; Hlady 1970:50, 51.)

75. Pipestone. MHS-A. 2929 (unworked block); MHS-M. 1274.A694 (small beads), 4178.E426 (large beads), 6875.2 (large pipe bowl), 1262.A682 (small pipe bowl).

76. Knife River flint. MHS-A. 11-65(3933.A2900), 12-135.

79. Canoe repair kit. NPS. 21CK6 1963 674-2; MHS-A. 21CK6 1936 uncatalogued (awls); MHS-M. 1981.70.11 (pitch). (Densmore 1979:149; A. Woolworth 1969a:71; 1969b:124.)

80. *Grand Panorama of London, from the Thames.* MHS-L.

81. Lead seals. MHS-A. 68.31, 64.228. (Wheeler et al. 1975:61, 62, 84, 85; Birk 1979:18, 19; 1975:81; Stone 1974:281.)

82. Baling needle. NPS. 21CK6 1970 1103. (Petersen 1964:47; Maxwell and Binford 1961:107; Stone 1974:158; A. Woolworth 1975:100, 108, 74A.)

83. *Casa da Fabrica da Tabaco.* (Arents 1937–1952:vol. 3 frontispiece; vol. 4 p. 147.)

84. Brazil tobacco. MHS-M. 1976.60. (Barbeau and Wilson 1944:36–39.)

85. *Sheffield from the Attercliffe Road.* (Hunter 1819:frontispiece.)

86. Knife blades. MHS-A. 21CK6 1936 uncatalogued. (A. Woolworth 1963a:219; Birk 1975:79.)

87. *The European Factories, Canton.* (Wright and Allom 1843:vol. 1 frontispiece.)

88. Vermilion. MHS-A. 64.228. (Wheeler et al. 1975:59, 62, 76; C. Hanson 1971:2.)

89. *View of Murano, the Seat of Glass Manufacture.* (Yriarte 1880:221.)

90. Venetian beads. MHS-M. 61.116.6. (Good 1977:28–31; Orchard 1929:88–90; Jenkins 1972:31–39; Woodward 1970:21.)

91. *Indians Carrying Food.* MHS-AV.

92. *Gathering Wild Rice.* (Eastman 1853:facing p. 50.)

93. Winnowing basket. MHS-M. 6935.20c. (Densmore 1979:128, plate 17.)

94. Ricing sticks. MHS-M. 6935.20a. (White 1980; Densmore 1979:128.)

95. *Indian Sugar Camp.* (Eastman 1853:facing p. 74.)

96. Copper kettle. MHS-M. 75.1. (Wheeler et al. 1975:59; Johnson 1956:50.)

97. Chain for a maple sugaring kettle. MHS-M. 64.117.b, c. (Densmore 1929:123; *Museum of the Fur Trade Quarterly* 1971c:6–9.)

98. Sugaring paddle and trough. MHS-M. 64.139.12, 7851.2.

(Densmore 1929:123; *Museum of the Fur Trade Quarterly* 1972c:6–9.)

99. *Spearing Fish in Winter.* (Eastman 1853:facing p. 62.)

100. Fishhooks. (*Museum of the Fur Trade Quarterly* 1980:8–11.)

101. Fish spear. NPS. 21CK6 1963 546-5. (Russell 1977:321–323; A. Woolworth 1969a:72, 109; 1969b:103.)

102. Bone fishing equipment. MHS-A. 388-9-4; MHS-M. 4377. (Stone 1974:158, 161; Brennan 1975:161, 172; Whiteford 1970:125, 128; Brower 1904:xx.)

103. Fishnet floats. MHS-M. 6874.43a–h. (Densmore 1979:154.)

104. Iron hoe. MHS-A. 21CK6 1936 487. (Russell 1977:342–348; Brain 1979:144–149; A. Woolworth 1963a:146, 147; 1963b:67, addenda.)

105. *Guarding the Corn Fields.* (Eastman 1853:facing p. 48; on L'Arbre Croche see Henry 1901:49, 54, 122.)

106. Mortar and pestle. MHS-M. 7059.50, 1981.70.12. (Wilson 1917:60–67.)

107. Scraper. MHS-M. 6935.30c. (Densmore 1979:163–165.)

108. Tanning paddle. MHS-M. 6935.30d. (Densmore 1979:164; Lyford 1943:97–101; Ritzenthaler 1947:8–11.)

109. Stretched beaver skin. (Hardy 1910:809.)

110. *Indians Preparing Hides.* MHS-AV.

111. Stretcher frames. MHS-M. uncatalogued. (Newhouse 1867:81.)

112. Tools for curing hides. MHS-M. 4080.A3024, 4071.A3015. (Buck and Ahenakew 1972:46–48; J. Hanson 1975:62; Brasser 1976:63; Brower 1904:114.)

113. *Montreal.* (Smyth 1842:n.p.)

114. Voyageur paddle. MHS-M. 7364. (Blegen 1943:21–23; Adney and Chapelle 1964:67.)

115. Trading license. (Laforge 1769:630.)

117. Voyageur engagement. (Moisan 1834.)

118. *Paddling.* (Scudder 1886:facing p. 38, 46.)

119. Sash. MHS-M. 68.97.1. (Barbeau 1937:6, 7, 25.)

120. Clay pipe. NPS. 21CK6 1963 688-1 (bowl), 21CK6 1964 972, 1668, 1669 (stem). (Nute 1931:50; Noël Hume 1976:296; A. Woolworth 1969b:126; 1969c:36, 51; for similar pipes from Michilimackinac see Stone 1974:146.)

121. Sash. MHS-M. 8976. (Barbeau 1937:6, 7; Brasser 1976:130; *Minnesota History News* 1964:3.)

122. *American Fur Co. Buildings, Fond du Lac. (Back View).* (McKenney 1827:facing p. 277.)

123. *Fur Traders at Yellow Lake, Wisconsin.* (Hölzlhuber 1965:49–64.)

124. *With the Fur Traders on Yellow Lake.* (Hölzlhuber 1965:49–64.)

125. *Ground Plat of the House on Lake Rouge.* B.177 a/1 fo 17d. (Hudson's Bay Company Archives, Provincial Archives of Manitoba.)

128. Scissors. NPS. 21CK6 1964 643. (A. Woolworth 1969a:51, 88; 1969c:21.)

129. Buckles. NPS. 21CK6 1963 204-4, 21CK6 1964 921. (A. Woolworth 1969a:64, 90; 1969b:40; 1969c:33.)

130. Dining utensils. NPS. 21CK6 1970 1085; MHS-A. 63.71.4; MHS-A. 9021.7(21CK6 1936 293). (A. Woolworth 1975:161, 162, 165, 71a; 1963b:40; Wheeler et al. 1975:64, 108; Massé 1921:152, 261; Cotterell 1967:34–36, 49, 162.)

131. Corkscrew. NPS. 21CK6 1964 901. (A. Woolworth 1969a:88; 1969b:32.)

132. Teakettle. MHS-A. uncatalogued. (Wheeler et al. 1975:37.)

133. Metal buttons. NPS. 21CK6 1963 127-3, 199-14, 255-2, 515-2, 550-50, 642-1; 21CK6 1964 499, 717, 1001, 1575, 1688, 1939. (A. Woolworth 1969a:52, 90, 94, 95, 117, 118; 1969b:21, 38, 51, 98, 105, 119; 1969c:16, 24, 36, 49, 51, 57; Olsen 1963:551–554; Woodward 1965:24–27.)

134. Shoe buckle frames. MHS-A. 63.67.1 (left); NPS. 21CK6 1964 1990 (top right), 21CK6 1970 846 (bottom right). (Wheeler et al. 1975:68, 95; Calver and Bolton 1950:56; Noël Hume 1976:84–86; A. Woolworth 1969a:55, 94; 1969c:59; 1975:90, 91, 142, 147, 55A.)

135. Spigot and valve collars. NPS. 21CK6 1970 1686, 190, 1462. (A. Woolworth 1975 : 180–183, 10A, 95A, 109A; Stone 1974 : 177–180.)
136. Keys. NPS. 21CK6 1963 688-2, 215-2, 235-4, 706-1, 284-1. (A. Woolworth 1969b : 42, 46, 57, 126, 130.)
137. Padlocks. MHS-A. uncatalogued; NPS. 21CK6 1970 695, 1852; 21CK6 1964 662. (I. Hart 1926 : 320–325; A. Woolworth 1975 : 90, 91, 171, 178, 44A, 121A; 1969a : 86, 87; 1969c : 22; Noël Hume 1976 : 251.)
138. Lock parts. MHS-A. 21CK6 1936 287 (top), uncatalogued (middle), 322, 321, 427 (bottom). (A. Woolworth 1963a : 160, 218; 1963b : 47, 61; I. Hart 1926 : 311–315, 323; Stone 1974 : 196.)
139. Door handle and latch. MHS-A. 21CK6 1937. (A. Woolworth 1963a : 142; 1963c : addenda.)
140. Keyhole escutcheons. NPS. 21CK6 1963 168-2; MHS-A. uncatalogued. (A. Woolworth 1969a : 71; 1969b : 31; I. Hart 1926 : 320–324; 1956 : 1–18.)
141. Hooks and hinged hasp. NPS. 21CK6 1970 755; MHS-A. 21CK6 1937 36-7; NPS. 21CK6 1970 400, 1356, 40. (H. Peterson 1964 : 16; A. Woolworth 1963a : 142; 1963c : 20; 1975 : 90, 112, 113, 169, 170, 178, 2A, 24A, 48A, 89A.)
142. *The Trading-Store.* (Ballantyne 1876 : 62.)
143. *Indians Bartering.* (Smyth 1842 : n.p.)
145. *The Indians giving a talk to Colonel Bouquet.* (W. Smith 1868.)
146. North West Company token. (Yeoman 1982 : 51.)
147. Currency. MHS-M. 4235.N109. (R. Gilman 1970 : 124–125; C. Hanson 1968 : 1–5; Nute 1928 : 287.)
148. Trading tokens. (Ray and Freeman 1978 : 54; C. Harding 1921 : 2–4.)
149. Inkwell. MHS-A. 21CK6 1937 25-2. (A. Woolworth 1963a : 135; 1963c : 13.)
150. Ledger page. MHS-MSS. Alexis Bailly Papers.
152. Steelyard. MHS-M. 6624.2. (*New England Mercantile Union Directory* 1849.)
153. Inventory of goods. MHS-MSS. Alexis Bailly Papers.
155. Inventory of furs. MHS-MSS. Alexis Bailly Papers.
157. Peace medal. MHS-M. 1979.18.3. (C. Gilman 1980 : 26–32; Prucha 1971 : xiv.)
158. Peace medal. MHS-M. 8407. (*Republican Eagle* 1965; Nute 1944 : 268–270; Prucha 1971 : 34, 48–50, 90–95.)
159. Peace medal. MHS-M. 6004. (Kvasnicka 1971 : 56–63; Prucha 1971 : 116; on Hole-in-the-Day see Nicolay 1977 : 82–91; on medals see also Fredrickson 1980 : 23–33, 79–86; Woodward 1970 : 25–27; J. Hanson 1975 : 85–90.)
160. Gorget. (Woodward 1970 : 33–37; Fredrickson 1980 : 31.)
161. Certificate of recognition. MHS-MSS. U.S. Office of Indian Affairs Papers. (Nute 1944 : 269.)
162. British flag. MHS-M. 1979.18.2. (C. Gilman 1980 : 26–32.)
169. *Fourreur.* (Diderot 1762–1772 : vol. 3, "Fourreur," plate V.)
170. The Wellington. (Martin 1892 : 125.)
171. Trade card. (Heal 1968 : plate XLIV.)
172. Man with a muff. (Boucher 1967 : 310.)
173. A hatter making felt. (Diderot 1762–1772 : vol. 2, part 1, "Chapelier," plate 1.)
174. Furrier's knife. MHS-M. 71.25. (Kebabian 1975 : n.p.; Ure 1872 : 838, 839.)
175. Hat block. MHS-M. 62.166.1. (Ure 1872 : 578; *Minneapolis City Directory* 1922 : 878.)
176. Paying respects. (Rameau 1931 : 14–24.)
178. Scraper made from a ceramic shard. MHS-M. 7059.202.
179. Fire steel. MHS-M. 2158.H437. (Hodge 1907 : 433; Hickerson 1974 : 263; Kvasnicka 1971 : 56–63; Densmore 1910 : 51; Upham and Dunlap 1912 : 42; J. Hanson 1975 : 68.)
180. Catlinite ornament mold. MHS-A. 3838.A2806. (G. Smith 1948 : 44–46; Alberts 1953 : 75, 76; for similar pipestone slabs see Killy 1948 : 48, 49, 51.)
181. Wire-wound pipestem. MHS-M. 6288.2. (West 1934 : plate 179.)
183. Stone and metal pipe bowls. MHS-M. 602.E180, 2160.E222. (West 1934 : 205, 246, 325, plates 173, 246, 247.)

184. War club. MHS-M. 304.E100. (H. Peterson 1965 : 8, 9, 88; J. Hanson 1975 : 35, 36; Brasser 1976 : 136; on Hall see Smalley 1896 : 285, 286.)
185. Powder flask and ornament cut from flask. NPS. 21CK6 1962 1926 (ornament); MHS-A. 2478.1236 (flask). (A. Woolworth 1968a : 41; 1968b : 50; Riling 1953 : 114, 284–286, 288.)
186. Hide flesher made from a gun barrel. MHS-M. 74.66.1. (C. Hanson 1955 : 24–27, 33, 40, 56, plate VIIIA; J. Hanson 1975 : 63, 64.)
187. Flesher made from a gun barrel. NPS. 21CK6 1970 1821. (A. Woolworth 1975 : 98, 118A.)
188. Musket balls. MHS-A. 63.65.1. (Wheeler et al. 1975 : 74.)
189. Pipe bowl. MHS-M. 69.41.8.
190. Pipe bowl. MHS-M. 288.E146.
191. Ceremonial club. MHS-M. 9666.9. (Brasser 1976 : 39; Casagrande and Ringheim 1980 : 21–23; J. Hanson 1975 : 85.)
192. Fishnet sinker. NPS. 21CK6 1963 54-5. (A. Woolworth 1969a : 73.)
193. Altered lead seals. MHS-A. 21CK6 1937 32-2 (center), 21CK6 1936 301-1 (left), 388-45-3 (right). (A. Woolworth 1963a : 166, 167; 1963b : 43; Calver and Bolton 1950 : 78; Stone 1974 : 154.)
194. Fire steel made from a file. MHS-M. 7059.220. (*Museum of the Fur Trade Quarterly* 1971b : 2–4; Russell 1977 : 353; J. Hanson 1975 : 68.)
195. Files. MHS-A. F.P.280, 261, 270. (Wheeler et al. 1975 : 59, 60, 62, 99, 102.)
196. Flesher made from a file. MHS-M. 6935.30b.
197. File-burned pipestem. MHS-M. 2857.E288. (H. Peterson 1965 : 38.)
198. Chisel made from a file. MHS-A. 4718. (Brower 1901 : 49.)
199. Patched kettle. MHS-A. 67.230.177.
200. Brass ornamental discs. MHS-A. 2680.A1882. (Brennan 1975 : 161–165; C. Brown 1918 : 96, 97; Mitchell 1908 : 305, 313.)
201. Scraps of kettles. MHS-A. 353-3-76, 65.68.12. (Birk 1981 : personal communication.)
202. Pouch with tinkling cones. MHS-M. 7891.3, 1981.70.8; NPS. 21CK6 1963 253-12. (J. Hanson 1975 : 75, 77; Woodward 1965 : 15; Briggs et al. 1939 : 11–17.)
203. Projectile points of kettle metal. NPS. 21CK6 1963 182-2; MHS-A. 388-50-32. (A. Woolworth 1969b : 34; Birk 1981 : personal communication.)
204. Knife made from a kettle scrap. MHS-A. 4070.A3014. (Brower 1904.)
205. Scraps cut from kettle metal. NPS. 21CK6 1963 200-20, 200-21, 200-22, 250-13, 305-2, 307-6, 646-4, 692-16 (diamonds), 250-10 (heart), 307-5 (octagon); MHS-M. 4401 (beads). (A. Woolworth 1969b : 39, 49, 61, 62, 119, 127; Brower 1904; Brain 1979 : 195.)
206. Woolen hood. MHS-M. 6935.33. (Densmore 1979 : 31, 33; Brasser 1976 : 173; for similar hoods see Peter Rindisbacher's watercolor of Cree Indians near York Factory, Public Archives of Canada.)
207. Woolen shirt. MHS-M. 8303.1.
208. Woolen leggings. MHS-M. 8303.1. (On ready-made clothing see Dechêne 1974 : 153, 154.)
209. Cloth belt. MHS-M. 8303.5. (On the "vertical-horizontal" beadwork technique see Lyford 1943 : 127, 128.)
210. Woven sash. MHS-M. 6091.3. (Barbeau 1937 : 12, 13.)
211. Pipe bag. MHS-M. 6037.3.
212. Sash. MHS-M. 6091.1.
213. *Reyse Door Nieuwe Ondekte Landen.* (Hennepin 1698 : frontispiece.)
214. Spoon locket. MHS-M. 68.210. (Fredrickson 1980 : 99; Alberts 1953 : 92, 93, plate 3G; Nute 1930 : 372.)
215. Real and imitation wampum. MHS-M. 8027.8; MHS-A. 63.65.6g. (Armour 1977 : 16–21.)
216. Glass beads and dentalium shells. MHS-M. 4278, 1981.70.10. (Orchard 1929 : 19, 20; Whiteford 1970 : 133; Kidd 1970 : 50, 51, 53.)
217. Gorget. (Fredrickson 1980 : 59.)

218. Brooch. (Fredrickson 1980 : 49–55; Langdon 1966 : 109.)
219. Silver armband. MHS-M. 1291.A711.
220. Silver cross. MHS-M. 347.A66. (Fredrickson 1980 : 36; Barbeau 1942 : 10–14.)
221. Beaver pendant. MHS-M. 74.66.2. (Cleland 1971 : 42, 43; Barbeau 1940 : 31, 32; Quimby 1966 : 95; Ensko 1937 : 31; C. Brown 1918 : 96.)
222. Hair plate. MHS-M. 6003.10. (J. Hanson 1975 : 93–96; C. Hanson 1981 : 1–8; on Ingersoll see Johnston 1980 : 122–132.)
223. Pipe tomahawk. MHS-M. 75.51.2. (H. Peterson 1965 : 118, 122, figs. 187, 207.)
224. Pipe tomahawk. MHS-M. 6167.4. (H. Peterson 1965 : 33–39; Woodward 1970 : 45; *Minnesota History* 1922 : 274.)
225. Crooked knife. MHS-M. 6935.32v. (C. Hanson 1975 : 5–9; Russell 1977 : 216–218.)

226. Matting needle. MHS-M. 565.A80. (Densmore 1979 : 157; Russell 1977 : 316.)
227. Quill flattener. MHS-M. 68.97.4. (Orchard 1916 : 8, 9; Neuman 1960 : 99–102; J. Hanson 1975 : 66; Lyford 1943 : 120–123.)
228. Pewter pipe bowl. MHS-A. 63.65.9. (Wheeler et al. 1975 : 75; Cleland 1971 : 86; West 1934 : 205, 325, plates 115, 246.)
229. Northwest trade gun. MHS-M. 1979.23.
232. Mirror. MHS-M. 4414. (Brower 1904.)
233. Blanket with ribbon appliqué. MHS-M. 6158.9. (Lyford 1943 : 34, 35; Fredrickson 1980 : 153.)
234. Yarn bag. MHS-M. 6874.20. (Densmore 1979 : 158–160; Lyford 1943 : 77–87.)
235. Hide coat. MHS-M. 8303.2. (Brasser 1976 : 40; 1975 : 52–57; Heilbron 1932 : 58, 145.)
236. Minnesota state seal. MHS-AV.

BIBLIOGRAPHY

ADNEY, EDWIN T. AND HOWARD I. CHAPELLE
1964   *The Bark Canoes and Skin Boats of North America.* (Bulletin 230.) Washington, D.C.: Smithsonian Institution.

ALBERTS, ROBERT C.
1953   "Trade Silver and Indian Silver Work in the Great Lakes Region," in *Wisconsin Archeologist*, 34:1–121 (March, 1953).

ARENTS, GEORGE
1937–52   *Tobacco, Its History Illustrated by The Books, Manuscripts and Engravings In the Library of George Arents, Jr.* 5 vols. New York: Rosenbach Co.

ARMOUR, DAVID A.
1977   "Beads in the Upper Great Lakes: A Study in Acculturation," in *Beads: Their Use by Upper Great Lakes Indians*, 10–26 (Publication No. 3.) Grand Rapids, Mich.: Public Museum.

ARTHUR, ELIZABETH
1973   *Thunder Bay District, 1821–1892.* Toronto: Champlain Society.

BALLANTYNE, ROBERT M.
1876   *Hudson Bay.* London: Thomas Nelson and Sons.

BARBEAU, MARIUS
1937   *Assomption Sash.* (Bulletin 93, Anthropological Series No. 24.) Ottawa: National Museum of Canada.
1940   "Indian Trade Silver," in Royal Society of Canada, *Proceedings and Transactions*, 3rd series, Section II, 30:27–41.
1942   "Indian Trade Silver," in *The Beaver*, December, 1942, p. 10–14.

BARBEAU, MARIUS AND CLIFFORD WILSON
1944   "Tobacco for the Fur Trade," in *The Beaver*, March, 1944, p. 36–39.

BARDON, RICHARD AND GRACE L. NUTE, EDS.
1947   "A Winter in the St. Croix Valley, 1802–03," in *Minnesota History*, 28:1–14, 142–159, 225–240 (March, June, and September, 1947).

BEAUBIEN, PAUL L.
1955   *Notes on the Archeology of Pipestone National Monument.* Omaha: National Park Service.

BIBEAU, DONALD F.
1981   "Fur Trade Literature from a Tribal Point of View," in Papers from the Fourth North American Fur Trade Conference, MHS–MSS.

BIRK, DOUGLAS A.
1975   "Recent Underwater Recoveries at Fort Charlotte, Grand Portage National Monument, Minnesota," in *International Journal of Nautical Archaeology and Underwater Exploration*, 4:73–84 (March, 1975).
1979   "Whitewater Archaeology," in *The Minnesota Volunteer*, May–June, 1979, p. 12–19.
1981   Unpublished study of the French fur trade in Minnesota, in the possession of the author.

BIRK, DOUGLAS A. AND BRUCE M. WHITE
1979   "Who Wrote the Diary of 'Thomas Connor'? A Fur Trade Mystery," in *Minnesota History*, 46:170–188 (Spring, 1979).

BISHOP, CHARLES A.
1974   *The Northern Ojibwa and the Fur Trade.* Toronto: Holt, Rinehart, and Winston.

BLEGEN, THEODORE C.
1937   "Fort St. Charles and the Northwest Angle," in *Minnesota History*, 18:231–248 (September, 1937).

BLEGEN, THEODORE C., ED.
1943   "Armistice and War on the Minnesota Frontier," in *Minnesota History*, 24:11–25 (March, 1943).

BOUCHER, FRANÇOIS
1967   *20,000 Years of Fashion: The History of Costume and Personal Adornment.* New York: Harry N. Abrams.

BRAIN, JEFFREY P.
1979   *The Tunica Treasure.* Cambridge: Harvard University, Peabody Museum.

BRASSER, TED J.
1975   "Métis Artisans," in *The Beaver*, Autumn, 1975, p. 52–57.
1976   *Bo'Jou, Neejee!: Profiles of Canadian Indian Art.* Ottawa: National Museum of Man.

BRAY, EDMUND C. AND MARTHA C. BRAY, EDS.
1976   *Joseph N. Nicollet on the Plains and Prairies.* St. Paul: MHS.

BRAY, MARTHA C., ED.
1970   *The Journals of Joseph N. Nicollet.* St. Paul: MHS.

BRENNAN, LOUIS A.
1975   *Artifacts of Prehistoric America.* Harrisburg, Pa.: Stackpole Books.

BRIGGS, CHARLES W., ET AL.
1939   "Memorial to Haydn Samuel Cole," in *Memorial Services for Deceased Members, Ramsey County Bar*, 11–17. St. Paul: Ramsey County Bar.

BROWER, JACOB V.
1901   *Memoirs of Explorations in the Basin of the Mississippi*, Vol. 4, *Kathio.* St. Paul: H. L. Collins Co.
1904   *Memoirs of Explorations in the Basin of the Mississippi*, Vol. 8, *Mandan.* St. Paul: McGill–Warner Co.

BROWN, CHARLES E.
1918   "Indian Trade Implements and Ornaments," in *Wisconsin Archeologist*, 17:61–97 (September, 1918).

BROWN, JENNIFER S. H.
1980   *Strangers in Blood.* Vancouver: University of British Columbia Press.
1981   "Man in His Natural State: The Indian Worlds of George Nelson," in Papers from the Fourth North American Fur Trade Conference, MHS–MSS.

BUCK, RUTH M. AND EDWARD AHENAKEW
1972   "Tanning Hides," in *The Beaver*, Summer, 1972, p. 46–48.

BUCK, SOLON J.
1965   "The Story of Grand Portage," in Rhoda R. Gilman and June D. Holmquist, eds., *Selections from "Minnesota History,"* 26–38. St. Paul: MHS.

BURPEE, LAWRENCE J.
1931   "Grand Portage," in *Minnesota History*, 12:359–377 (December, 1931).

BURPEE, LAWRENCE J., ED.
1968   *Journals of La Vérendrye.* Reprint edition. New York: Greenwood Press.

CALVER, WILLIAM L. AND REGINALD P. BOLTON
1950   *History Written with Pick and Shovel.* New York: New-York Historical Society.

CAREY, A. MERWYN
1953   *American Firearms Makers.* New York: Thomas Y. Crowell Co.

CASAGRANDE, LOUIS B. AND MELISSA M. RINGHEIM
1980   *Straight Tongue: Minnesota Indian Art from the Bishop Whipple Collections.* St. Paul: Science Museum of Minnesota.

CATLIN, GEORGE
1848   *Catlin's Notes of Eight Years' Travels and Residence in Europe with His North American Indian Collection*, Vol. 2. London: Privately published.

CHILDS, HENRY W.
1905   "The Life and Work of General Sanborn," in *Minnesota Historical Collections*, 10:838–856.

CLELAND, CHARLES E.
1966   *The Prehistoric Animal Ecology and Ethnozoology of the Upper Great Lakes Region.* (Anthropological Paper No. 29.) Ann Arbor: University of Michigan, Museum of Anthropology.

1971   *The Lasanen Site.* (Anthropological Series, Vol. 1, No. 1, Publications of the Museum.) East Lansing: Michigan State University.

1972   "From Sacred to Profane: Style Drift in the Decoration of Jesuit Finger Rings," in *American Antiquity*, 37:202–210 (April, 1972).

COE, RALPH T.
1977   *Sacred Circles: Two Thousand Years of North American Indian Art.* Kansas City, Mo.: Nelson Gallery of Art–Atkins Museum of Fine Arts.

COPWAY, GEORGE
1860   *Indian Life and Indian History.* Boston: Albert Colby and Co.

COTTERELL, HOWARD H.
1967   *Old Pewter: Its Makers and Marks.* Reprint edition. Rutland, Vt.: Charles E. Tuttle Co.

COUES, ELLIOTT M., ED.
1897   *New Light on the Early History of the Greater Northwest.* Vol. 1. New York: Francis P. Harper.

DECHÊNE, LOUISE
1974   *Habitants et Marchands de Montréal au XVIIᵉ Siècle.* Paris: Librairie Plon.

DEETZ, JAMES
1977   *In Small Things Forgotten.* Garden City, N.Y.: Anchor Books.

DE LOTBINIERE, SEYMOUR
1980   "English Gunflint Making in the Seventeenth and Eighteenth Centuries," in *Minnesota Archaeologist*, 39:55–69 (May, 1980).

DENSMORE, FRANCES
1910   *Chippewa Music.* (Bureau of American Ethnology, Bulletin 45.) Washington, D.C.: Smithsonian Institution.

1928   "Uses of Plants by the Chippewa Indians," in Bureau of American Ethnology, *Annual Report No. 44*, 275–397. Washington, D.C.: Smithsonian Institution.

1979   *Chippewa Customs.* Reprint edition. St. Paul: MHS.

DIDEROT, DENIS
1762–72 *Encyclopédie, ou Dictionnaire Raisonné des Sciences, des Arts et des Métiers: Recueil de Planches.* 11 vols. Paris.

DIXON, GEORGE
1980   "Belville Looks Backwards," in *Minnesota Monthly*, June, 1980, p. 41–42.

DOUGLAS, FREDERIC H.
1941   *Birchbark and the Indian.* (Leaflet No. 102.) Denver: Denver Art Museum.

DU CREUX, FRANÇOIS
1951   *History of Canada or New France*, Vol. 1. Reprint edition. Toronto: Champlain Society.

DUNHILL, ALFRED
1924   *The Pipe Book.* Toronto: Macmillan Company of Canada.

EASTMAN, MARY H.
1853   *The American Aboriginal Portfolio.* Philadelphia: Lippincott, Grambo & Co.

ECCLES, W. J.
1969   *The Canadian Frontier 1534–1760.* New York: Holt, Rinehart, and Winston.

ENGAGEMENTS OF VOYAGEURS
1687–1777 Photocopies of Selected Documents from Montreal Judicial Archives, Box 2, Marie Gerin-Lajoie Collection, MHS–MSS.

ENSKO, STEPHEN G. C.
1937   *American Silversmiths and Their Marks II.* New York: Robert Ensko, Inc.

FADEN, WILLIAM
1777   *North American Atlas.* London: W. Faden.

FERGUSON, JAMES C.
1954   "Reminiscences," in Ferguson Papers, MHS–MSS.

FOLWELL, WILLIAM W.
1922   *A History of Minnesota*, Vol. 1. St. Paul: MHS.

FREDRICKSON, N. JAYE AND SANDRA GIBBS
1980   *The Covenant Chain.* Ottawa: National Museums of Canada.

GATES, CHARLES M., ED.
1965   *Five Fur Traders of the Northwest.* St. Paul: MHS.

GILMAN, CAROLYN
1980   "Grand Portage Ojibway Indians Give British Medals to Historical Society," in *Minnesota History*, 47:26–32 (Spring, 1980).

GILMAN, RHODA R.
1970   "Last Days of the Upper Mississippi Fur Trade," in *Minnesota History*, 42:123–140 (Winter, 1970).

GOOD, MARY E.
1977   "Glass Bead Manufacturing Techniques," in *Beads: Their Use by Upper Great Lakes Indians*, 28–34 (Publication No. 3) Grand Rapids, Mich.: Public Museum.

HAMILTON, T. M., ET AL.
1980   *Colonial Frontier Guns.* Chadron, Neb.: The Fur Press.

HANSON, CHARLES E., JR.
1955   *The Northwest Gun.* (Publication in Anthropology No. 2) Lincoln: Nebraska State Historical Society.

1968   "Trade Notes and Tokens," in *Museum of the Fur Trade Quarterly*, Spring, 1968, p. 1–5.

1971   "A Paper of Vermilion," in *Museum of the Fur Trade Quarterly*, Fall, 1971, p. 1–3.

1975   "The Crooked Knife," in *Museum of the Fur Trade Quarterly*, Summer, 1975, p. 5–10.

1981   "Plains Indian Hair Plates," in *Museum of the Fur Trade Quarterly*, Summer, 1981, p. 1–8.

HANSON, JAMES A.
1972   "Upper Missouri Arrow Points," in *Museum of the Fur Trade Quarterly*, Winter, 1972, p. 2–8.

1975   *Metal Weapons, Tools, and Ornaments of the Teton Dakota Indians.* Lincoln: University of Nebraska Press.

HARDING, ARTHUR R.
1907   *Steel Traps.* Columbus, Ohio: A. R. Harding Publishing Co.

HARDING, CHRIS
1921   "The Monetary System of the Far Fur Country," in *The Beaver*, June, 1921, p. 2–4.

HARDY, MANLY
1910   "A Fall Fur Hunt in Maine," in *Forest and Stream*, 74:768–770, 808–811 (May 14, 21, 1910).

HART, EVAN A.
1963   "Rare Trade Cross—Lost and Found," in *Minnesota History News*, December, 1963, p. 2–3.

HART, IRVING H.
1926   "The Site of the Northwest Company Post on Sandy Lake," in *Minnesota History*, 7:311–325 (December, 1926).

1956   "An Amateur Archaeologist in Northern Minnesota," in *Minnesota Archaeologist*, April, 1956, p. 1–18.

HEAL, AMBROSE
1968   *London Tradesmen's Cards of the XVIII Century.* Reprint edition. New York: Dover Publications.

HEIDENREICH, CONRAD AND ARTHUR J. RAY
1976   *The Early Fur Trades: A Study in Cultural Interaction.* Toronto: McClelland and Stewart.

HEILBRON, BERTHA L., ED.
1932   *With Pen and Pencil on the Frontier.* St. Paul: MHS.

HENNEPIN, LOUIS
1698   *Aenmerckelycke Historische Reys-Beschryvinge Door verscheyde Landen veel grooter als die van geheel Europa onlanghs ontdeckt.* Utrecht: Anthony Schouten.

HENNESSY, W. B.
1906   *Past and Present of St. Paul, Minnesota.* Chicago: S. J. Clarke.

HENRY, ALEXANDER
1901   *Travels & Adventures in Canada and the Indian Territories.* Reprint edition. Boston: Little, Brown, & Co.

HICKERSON, HAROLD, ED.
1959   "Journal of Charles Jean-Baptiste Chaboillez," in *Ethnohistory,* 6:265–316, 363–427 (Summer, Fall, 1959).

HICKERSON, HAROLD
1974   *Chippewa Indians II: Ethnohistory of Mississippi Bands and Pillager and Winnibigoshish Bands of Chippewa.* New York: Garland Publishing.

HINCKLEY, C. T.
1853   "Everyday Actualities. No. VIII: The Manufacture of Gas and Gas-Fixtures," in *Godey's Lady's Book,* 46:197–203 (March, 1853).

HLADY, WALTER M., ED.
1970   *Ten Thousand Years: Archaeology in Manitoba.* Winnipeg: Manitoba Archaeological Society.

HODGE, FREDERICK W., ED.
1907   *Handbook of American Indians North of Mexico,* Vol. 1. Washington, D.C.: Smithsonian Institution.

HOLMQUIST, JUNE D. AND JEAN A. BROOKINS
1972   *Minnesota's Major Historic Sites.* Revised edition. St. Paul: MHS.

HÖLZLHUBER, FRANZ
1965   "Sketches from Northwestern America and Canada," in *American Heritage,* June, 1965, p. 49–64.

HUNT, GEORGE T.
1940   *The Wars of the Iroquois: A Study in Intertribal Trade Relations.* Madison: University of Wisconsin Press.

HUNTER, JOSEPH
1819   *Hallamshire. The History and Topography of the Parish of Sheffield in the County of York.* London: Lackington, Hughes, Harding, Mavor, and Jones.

INNIS, HAROLD A.
1973   *The Fur Trade in Canada: An Introduction to Canadian Economic History.* Revised edition. Toronto: University of Toronto Press.

JACKSON, MARJORIE G.
1930   "The Beginning of British Trade at Michilimackinac," in *Minnesota History,* 11:231–270 (September, 1930).

JACOBS, WILBUR R.
1972   *Dispossessing the American Indian.* New York: Charles Scribner's Sons.

JENKINS, MICHAEL R.
1972   "Trade Beads in Alaska," in *Alaska Journal,* Summer, 1972, p. 31–39.

JOHNSON, A. M.
1956   "Mons. Maugenest Suggests. . . ," in *The Beaver,* Summer, 1956, p. 49–53.

JOHNSTON, PATRICIA C.
1980   "Truman Ingersoll: St. Paul Photographer Pictures the World," in *Minnesota History,* 47:122–132 (Winter, 1980).

KAUFFMAN, HENRY J.
1968   *American Copper & Brass.* Camden, N.J.: Thomas Nelson and Sons.

KAVANAGH, MARTIN
1967   *La Vérendrye: His Life and Times.* Brandon, Man.: Privately published.

KEBABIAN, JOHN S., ED.
1975   Joseph Smith, *Explanation or Key, to the Various Manufactories of Sheffield.* South Burlington, Vt.: Early American Industries Association.

KELLOGG, LOUISE P.
1925   *The French Régime in Wisconsin and the Northwest.* Madison: State Historical Society of Wisconsin.

1931   "The French Regime in the Great Lakes Country," in *Minnesota History,* 12:347–358 (December, 1931).

KIDD, KENNETH E. AND MARTHA ANN KIDD
1970   "A Classification System for Glass Beads for the Use of Field Archaeologists," in *Canadian Historic Sites: Occasional Papers in Archaeology and History, No. 1,* 45–89. Ottawa: National Historic Sites Service.

KILLY, MONROE P.
1948   "Some Minnesota Catlinite Objects," in *Minnesota Archaeologist,* 14:48–51 (April, 1948).

KVASNICKA, ROBERT M.
1971   "From the Wilderness to Washington— and Back Again," in *Kansas Quarterly,* 3:56–63 (Fall, 1971).

LAFORGE, VINCENT
1769   License to trade, August 16, 1769, in RG4, B28, vol. 11, p. 630–633, Public Archives of Canada, Ottawa.

LAHONTAN, LOUIS-ARMAND, BARON DE
1905   *New Voyages to North-America.* 2 vols. Reprint edition. Chicago: A. C. McClurg and Co.

LAMB, W. KAYE, ED.
1957   *Sixteen Years in the Indian Country: The Journal of Daniel Williams Harmon 1800–1816.* Toronto: Macmillan Company of Canada.

1970   *Journals and Letters of Sir Alexander Mackenzie.* Glasgow: Cambridge University Press.

LANGDON, JOHN E.
1966   *Canadian Silversmiths 1700–1900.* Toronto: Stinehour Press.

LASS, WILLIAM E.
1980   *Minnesota's Boundary with Canada.* St. Paul: MHS.

LE BEAU, CLAUDE
1738   *Avantures . . . ou, Voyage Curieux et Nouveau, Parmi les Sauvages de l'Amerique Septentrionale.* Amsterdam: H. Uytwerf.

LEGARDEUR, PIERRE
1886   "Memoir," in Public Archives of Canada, *Report,* 1886, p. clix–clxix.

LONGFELLOW, HENRY W.
1855   *The Song of Hiawatha.* Boston: Ticknor and Fields.

LYFORD, CARRIE A.
1943   *The Crafts of the Ojibwa (Chippewa).* Phoenix, Ariz.: Phoenix Indian School.

MACFIE, JOHN
1962   "A Short River Reveals Evidence of Its Long History," in *The Beaver,* Winter, 1962, p. 48–51.

McKENNEY, THOMAS
1827   *Sketches of a Tour to the Lakes.* Baltimore: Fielding Lucas, Jr.

McKENZIE, CHARLES
1809   "Some account of the Mississouri Indians in the years 1804, 5, 6 and 7," rare book department, McGill University Library, Montreal.

McKENZIE, RODERICK
1805   "Conseils au Voyageur intelligent et instruit," in *Masson Collection,* Vol. 38. Ottawa: Public Archives of Canada.

n.d.   "Some account of the North West Company containing Analogy of Nations," in *Masson Collection,* Vol. 44, Part 3. Ottawa: Public Archives of Canada.

MARGRY, PIERRE, ED.
1886   *Decouvertes et Etablissements des Francais.* Vol. 6. Paris: Jouaust et Sigaux.

MARTIN, HORACE T.
1892   *Castorologia.* Montreal: William Drysdale and Co. London: Edward Stanford.

Marx, Karl
1967   *Capital*. New York: International Publishers.
Massé, Henri J. L. J.
1921   *The Pewter Collector*. New York: Dodd, Mead and Co.
Masson, Louis R., ed.
1960   *Les Bourgeois de La Compagnie du Nord-Ouest*. Reprint edition. New York: Antiquarian Press.
Maxwell, Moreau S. and Lewis H. Binford
1961   *Excavation at Fort Michilimackinac, Mackinac City, Michigan, 1959 Season*. Lansing: Michigan State University.
Megill, Doris K.
1963   "Underwater Finds in the French River," in *Canadian Geographical Journal*, 67:48–53 (August, 1963).
Metcalf, George
1966   "A Green River Knife and Sheath From the Southern Plains," in *Museum of the Fur Trade Quarterly*, Summer, 1966, p. 4–6.
M'Gillivray, Duncan
1928   "Some Account of the Trade Carried on by the North West Company," in Public Archives of Canada, *Report*, 1928, p. 58–73.
Minneapolis City Directory
1922
Minnesota History
1922   "Accessions," 4:272–277 (February–May, 1922).
1924   "Accessions," 5:503–511 (August, 1924).
1931   "Historical Exploring in the 'Arrowhead Country'," 12:281–296 (September, 1931).
1972   "Society Collects Animal Traps," 43:146–148 (Winter, 1972).
Minnesota History News
1964   "Codere Death a Loss to Society," May, 1964, p. 3.
Mitchell, Edward C.
1908   "Archaeological Collections Recently Donated to This Society," in *Minnesota Historical Collections*, 12:305–318.
Moisan, Etienne
1834   Contract with Gabriel Franchere, Henry H. Sibley Papers, MHS–MSS.
Molloy, John T.
1976   *Dress for Success*. New York: Warner Books.
Montaigne, Michel de
1958   *Essais*. Vol. 1. Paris: Editions Garnier.
1978   *Essays*. Translated by J. M. Cohen. Middlesex: Penguin Books.
Montesquieu, Charles L.
1980   *Persian Letters*. Reprint edition. Middlesex: Penguin Books.
Morantz, Toby
1980   "The Fur Trade and the Cree of James Bay," in Carol M. Judd and Arthur J. Ray, eds., *Old Trails and New Directions*, 39–58. Toronto: University of Toronto Press.
Morse, Eric W.
1969   *Fur Trade Canoe Routes of Canada / Then and Now*. Ottawa: Queen's Printer.
Morse, Richard F.
1857   "The Chippewas of Lake Superior," in *Wisconsin Historical Collections*, 3:338–369.
Museum of the Fur Trade Quarterly
1971a   "Indian Awls," Summer, 1971, p. 2–3.
1971b   "Trade Fire Steels," Winter, 1971, p. 2–4.
1971c   "Maple Sugar in the Fur Trade," Spring, 1971, p. 6–9.
1980   "Fish Hooks," Winter, 1980, p. 8–11.
Nelson, George
n.d.   "Reminiscences," in George Nelson Collection, Toronto Public Library.
Neuman, Robert W.
1960   "Porcupine Quill Flatteners from Central United States," in *American Antiquity*, 26:99–102 (July, 1960).

New England Mercantile Union Directory
1849   New York: L.C. and H.L. Pratt and Co.
Newhouse, Sewell
1867   *The Trapper's Guide*. Wallingford, Conn.: Oneida Community.
Nicolay, John G.
1977   "Hole-in-the-Day," in *Minnesota Archaeologist*, 36:82–91 (July, 1977).
Noël Hume, Ivor
1976   *A Guide to Artifacts of Colonial America*. New York: Alfred A. Knopf.
Nute, Grace L.
1928   "Beaver Money," in *Minnesota History*, 9:287–288 (September, 1928).
1930   "Posts in the Minnesota Fur-Trading Area, 1660–1855," in *Minnesota History*, 11:353–385 (December, 1930).
1931   *The Voyageur*. New York and London: D. Appleton.
1940   "A British Legal Case and Old Grand Portage," in *Minnesota History*, 21:117–148 (June, 1940).
1941   *The Voyageur's Highway*. St. Paul: MHS.
1944   "Indian Medals and Certificates," in *Minnesota History*, 25:265–270 (September, 1944).
1950   *Rainy River Country*. St. Paul: MHS.
1951   "Marin versus La Vérendrye," in *Minnesota History*, 32:226–238 (December, 1951).
Olsen, Stanley J.
1963   "Dating Early Plain Buttons by Their Form," in *American Antiquity*, 28:551–554 (April, 1963).
Orchard, William C.
1916   *The Technique of Porcupine-Quill Decoration Among the North American Indians*. (Contributions, Vol. 4, No. 1.) New York: Museum of the American Indian, Heye Foundation.
1929   *Beads and Beadwork of the American Indians*. (Contributions, Vol. 11.) New York: Museum of the American Indian, Heye Foundation.
Parker, Donald D., ed.
1966   *The Recollections of Philander Prescott*. Lincoln: University of Nebraska Press.
Parker, John, ed.
1976   *The Journals of Jonathan Carver and Related Documents, 1766–1770*. St. Paul: MHS.
Peirce, Parker I.
1962   *Antelope Bill*. Reprint edition. Minneapolis: Ross and Haines.
Petersen, Eugene T.
1964   *Gentlemen on the Frontier*. Mackinac Island, Mich.: Mackinac Island State Park Commission.
Peterson, Harold L.
1958   *American Knives*. New York: Charles Scribner's Sons.
1964   "Trade Guns," in *Encyclopedia of Firearms*. New York: E. P. Dutton.
1965   *American Indian Tomahawks*. (Contributions, Vol. 19.) New York: Museum of the American Indian, Heye Foundation.
Peterson, Jacqueline
1978   "Prelude to Red River: A Social Portrait of the Great Lakes Métis," in *Ethnohistory*, 25:41–67 (Winter, 1978).
Pioneer Press (St. Paul, Minn.)
1955   April 19, 1955, sec. 1, p. 4.
Prucha, Francis P.
1971   *Indian Peace Medals in American History*. Reprint edition. Lincoln: University of Nebraska Press.
Prud'homme, L. A.
1916   *Pierre Gaultier de Varennes sieur de la Vérendrye*. (Bulletin, Vol. 5, Part 2.) St. Boniface, Man.: Historical Society of St. Boniface.
Quimby, George I.
1966   *Indian Culture and European Trade Goods*. Madison: University of Wisconsin Press.

RAMEAU, PIERRE
1931   *The Dancing Master.* Reprint edition. London: C. W. Beaumont.

RAY, ARTHUR J.
1974   *Indians in the Fur Trade.* Toronto: University of Toronto Press.

RAY, ARTHUR J. AND DONALD FREEMAN
1978   *"Give Us Good Measure."* Toronto: University of Toronto Press.

RENFREW, COLIN
1975   "Trade as Action at a Distance: Questions of Integration and Communication," in Jeremy A. Sabloff and C. C. Lamberg-Karlovsky, eds., *Ancient Civilization and Trade,* 3–59. Albuquerque: University of New Mexico Press.

Republican Eagle (Red Wing, Minn.)
1965   April 30, 1965, p. 2.

RICH, EDWIN E.
1966   *Montreal and the Fur Trade.* Montreal: McGill University Press.

RILING, RAY
1953   *The Powder Flask Book.* New Hope, Pa.: Robert Halter, The River House.

RITZENTHALER, ROBERT
1947   "The Chippewa Indian Method of Securing and Tanning Deerskin," in *Wisconsin Archeologist,* 28:6–13 (March, 1947).

ROLETTE, JOSEPH
1835   Letter to Ramsay Crooks, January 20, 1835, American Fur Company Papers, New-York Historical Society, microfilm copy in MHS–MSS.

ROSE, ARTHUR P.
1911   *An Illustrated History of the Counties of Rock and Pipestone Minnesota.* Luverne, Minn.: Northern History Publishing Co.

RUSSELL, CARL P.
1957   *Guns on the Early Frontiers.* Berkeley and Los Angeles: University of California Press.

1977   *Firearms, Traps, & Tools of the Mountain Men.* Reprint edition. Albuquerque: University of New Mexico Press.

SAUM, LEWIS O.
1965   *The Fur Trader and the Indian.* Seattle: University of Washington Press.

SCUDDER, SAMUEL H.
1886   *The Winnipeg Country or Roughing it with an Eclipse Party.* Boston: Cupples, Upham, & Co.

SMALLEY, EUGENE V.
1896   *A History of the Republican Party.* St. Paul: Privately published.

SMART, CHRISTOPHER, ET AL., COMPS.
1760   *The World Displayed; or a Curious Collection of Voyages and Travels,* Vol. 5. London: J. Newbery.

SMITH, G. HUBERT
1948   "An Ornament-Mold From Minnesota," in *Minnesota Archaeologist,* 14:44–46 (April, 1948).

1980   *Explorations of the La Vérendryes in the Northern Plains 1738–43.* Lincoln: University of Nebraska Press.

SMITH, WILLIAM
1868   *Historical Account of Bouquet's Expedition Against the Ohio Indians in 1764.* Reprint edition. Cincinnati, Ohio: Robert Clarke and Co.

SMYTH, COKE
1842   *Sketches in the Canadas.* London: Th. McLean.

STEVENS, WAYNE E.
1928   *The Northwest Fur Trade, 1763–1800.* Urbana: University of Illinois Press.

STONE, LYLE M.
1974   *Fort Michilimackinac 1715–1781.* (Anthropological Series, Vol. 2, Publications of the Museum.) East Lansing: Michigan State University in cooperation with Mackinac Island State Park Commission.

SULTE, BENJAMIN
1896   "Pierre Boucher et son Livre," in Royal Society of Canada, *Proceedings and Transactions,* Second Series, Vol. 2.

TANNER, ADRIAN
1979   *Bringing Home Animals.* New York: St. Martin's Press.

TANNER, JOHN
1956   *A Narrative of the Captivity and Adventures of John Tanner.* Reprint edition. Minneapolis: Ross and Haines.

TEGEDER, ROBERT M.
1979   *Rediscovery and Restoration of Fort St. Charles.* Collegeville, Minn.: St. John's Abbey Press.

THOMPSON, ERWIN N.
1969   *Grand Portage.* Washington, D.C.: NPS, Office of Archeology and Historic Preservation, Division of History.

TURNER, FREDERICK J.
1977   *The Character and Influence of the Indian Trade in Wisconsin.* Norman: University of Oklahoma Press.

UNITED STATES CENSUS
1894   *Report on Indians Taxed and Indians Not Taxed . . . at the Eleventh Census: 1890.* Washington, D.C.: Census Office, Department of the Interior.

UPHAM, WARREN AND ROSE B. DUNLAP
1912   *Minnesota Biographies 1655–1912.* (Minnesota Historical Collections, Vol. 14.) St. Paul: MHS.

URE, ANDREW
1872   *Ure's Dictionary of Arts, Manufactures and Mines,* Vol. 2. Sixth edition. London: Longmans, Green, and Co.

VAN KIRK, SYLVIA
1980   *"Many Tender Ties."* Winnipeg: Watson and Dwyer.

1981   "George Nelson's Wretched Career, 1802–1823," in Papers from the Fourth North American Fur Trade Conference, MHS–MSS.

VERNON, ROBERT AND LEROY GONSIOR
1978   "On the Definition and Manufacture of French Gunflints: Evidence from Historic Fort Snelling," in *Minnesota Archaeologist,* 37:33–47 (February, 1978).

WALLACE, W. STEWART, ED.
1934   *Documents Relating to the North West Company.* Toronto: Champlain Society.

WARREN, WILLIAM W.
1885   "History of the Ojibways," in *Minnesota Historical Collections,* 5:21–394.

WEST, GEORGE A.
1934   *Tobacco, Pipes and Smoking Customs of the American Indians.* (Bulletin, Vol. 17.) Milwaukee: Public Museum of the City of Milwaukee.

WHEELER, ROBERT C., ET AL.
1975   *Voices from the Rapids.* St. Paul: MHS.

WHITE, BRUCE M., COMP.
1977   *The Fur Trade in Minnesota: An Introductory Guide to Manuscript Sources.* St. Paul: MHS.

WHITE, BRUCE M.
1980   "La Folle Avoine: The St. Croix Fur Trade," in *The Dalles Visitor* (Taylors Falls), Summer, 1980.

1981   "Give Us a Little Milk: The Social and Cultural Meanings of Gift Giving in the Lake Superior Trade," in Papers from the Fourth North American Fur Trade Conference, MHS–MSS.

WHITEFORD, ANDREW H.
1970   *North American Indian Arts.* New York: Golden Press.

WILLIAMS, J. FLETCHER
1876   *History of the City of Saint Paul.* (Minnesota Historical Collections, Vol. 4.) St. Paul: MHS.

WILLIAMS, MENTOR L.
1974   *Schoolcraft's Indian Legends.* Reprint edition. Westport, Conn.: Greenwood Press.

WILSON, GILBERT L.
1917   *Agriculture of the Hidatsa Indians.* (Studies in the

Social Sciences, No. 9.) Minneapolis: University of Minnesota.

WINCHELL, NEWTON H.

1911 *The Aborigines of Minnesota*. St. Paul: Pioneer Co.

WITTHOFT, JOHN

1966 "A History of Gunflints," in *Pennsylvania Archaeologist*, 36: 12–49 (June, 1966).

WOODWARD, ARTHUR

1965 *Indian Trade Goods*. (Publication No. 2.) Portland: Oregon Archaeological Society.

1970 *The Denominators of the Fur Trade: An Anthology of Writings on the Material Culture of the Fur Trade*. Pasadena, Cal.: Socio-Technical Publications.

WOOLWORTH, ALAN R.

1963a "Archeological Excavations at the Northwest Company's Fur Trade Post, Grand Portage, Minnesota, in 1936–1937 by the Minnesota Historical Society." Unpublished, typewritten report prepared for the NPS.

1963b "Catalogue of Objects Found at Grand Portage in the Course of Excavation, 1936." Unpublished, typewritten report prepared for the NPS.

1963c "Catalogue of Objects Found at Grand Portage in the Course of Excavation, 1937." Unpublished, typewritten report prepared for the NPS.

1968a "Archeological Excavations at Grand Portage National Monument, 1962 Field Season." Unpublished, typewritten report prepared for the NPS.

1968b "Archeological Catalog, Grand Portage National Monument, 1962." Unpublished, typewritten report prepared for the NPS.

1969a "Archaeological Excavations at Grand Portage National Monument, 1963–1964 Field Seasons." Unpublished, typewritten report prepared for the NPS.

1969b "Archaeological Catalog, Grand Portage National Monument, 1963." Unpublished, typewritten report prepared for the NPS.

1969c "Archaeological Catalog, Grand Portage National Monument, 1964." Unpublished, typewritten report prepared for the NPS.

1975 "Archeological Excavations at the North West Company's Depot, Grand Portage, Minnesota, in 1970–1971 by the Minnesota Historical Society." Unpublished, typewritten report prepared for the NPS.

1980 "Boucher's 'Little Fort' and Mr. Mailloux's Establishment." Unpublished paper in the possession of the author.

1981 "Minnesota Historical Society Involvement with Grand Portage, Minnesota, 1922–1978." Unpublished paper in the possession of the author.

WOOLWORTH, NANCY L.

1965 "The Grand Portage Mission: 1731–1965," in *Minnesota History*, 39: 301–310 (Winter, 1965).

1975 "Grand Portage in the Revolutionary War," in *Minnesota History*, 44: 199–208 (Summer, 1975).

WOZNIAK, JOHN S.

1978 *Contact, Negotiation and Conflict*. Washington, D.C.: University Press of America.

WRIGHT, GEORGE N. AND THOMAS ALLOM

1843 *China, Its Scenery, Architecture, Social Habits, &c. Illustrated*. New York and London: London Printing and Publishing Co.

WYNN COMPANY, W. AND C.

1798–99 Sample Book, Vol. 3, in Essex Institute, Salem, Mass.

YEOMAN, RICHARD S.

1982 *A Guide Book of United States Coins*. 35th edition. Racine, Wis.: Western Publishing Co.

YRIARTE, CHARLES

1880 *Venice: Its History—Art—Industries and Modern Life*. London: George Bell and Sons.